Current
CONTROVERSIES

Vegetarianism

Other Books in the Current Controversies Series

Vegetarianism

Debra A. Miller, Book Editor

GREENHAVEN PRESS

A part of Gale, Cengage Learning

GALE
CENGAGE Learning™

Detroit • New York • San Francisco • New Haven, Conn • Waterville, Maine • London

Christine Nasso, *Publisher*
Elizabeth Des Chenes, *Managing Editor*

© 2010 Greenhaven Press, a part of Gale, Cengage Learning

Articles in Greenhaven Press anthologies are often edited for length to meet page require-ments. In addition, original titles of these works are changed to clearly present the main thesis and to explicitly indicate the author's opinion. Every effort is made to ensure that Greenhaven Press accurately reflects the original intent of the authors. Every effort has been made to trace the owners of copyrighted material.

Cover image copyright Maram, 2010. Used under license from Shutterstock.com.

LIBRARY OF CONGRESS CATALOGING-IN-PUBLICATION DATA

Vegetarianism / Debra A. Miller, book editor.
    p. cm. -- (Current controversies)
  Includes bibliographical references and index.
  ISBN 978-0-7377-4925-0 (hardcover) -- ISBN 978-0-7377-4926-7 (pbk.)
  1. Vegetarianism--Juvenile literature. I. Miller, Debra A.
  TX392.V442 2010
  641.5'636--dc22
                                                    2010006725

Printed in the United States of America
1 2 3 4 5 6 7 14 13 12 11 10

Contents

Chapter 1: Is Vegetarianism Healthy?

Despite its potential health benefits, a long-term vegetarian diet can be dangerous unless attention is paid to getting balanced nutrition. Challenges include getting enough protein and B vitamins, making sure that you don't eat too many unhealthy sugary or processed foods, and avoiding dependence on carbohydrates, which can lead to weight gain.

Chapter 2: Is Vegetarianism Morally Superior to a Meat Diet?

Yes: Vegetarianism Is Morally Superior to a Meat Diet

Many Eastern religions, such as Hinduism and Buddhism, consider the killing and eating of sentient animals to be barbaric, but most Western religions do not hold the same vegetarian religious beliefs. Yet, Jesus himself may have been a vegetarian and vegetarianism likely was part of early Christian principles.

No: Vegetarianism Is Not Morally Superior to a Meat Diet

Chapter 3: Is Vegetarianism More Environmentally Sustainable Than a Meat Diet?

Yes: Vegetarianism Is More Environmentally Sustainable Than a Meat Diet

People who eat meat products generated by the livestock industry are helping to foul the air, water, and soil; contribute to global warming; and perpetuate the abuse of innocent and sentient animals. One's diet is therefore no longer a personal issue but a political one, and choosing vegetarianism is the most powerful way people can force the global meat industry to enact reforms.

No: Vegetarianism Is Not More Environmentally Sustainable Than a Meat Diet

Whether meat is bad for the environment depends on how and where the animals are raised and how the meat is used in the diet. If livestock are raised without contributing to deforestation, fed on naturally occurring vegetation and non-fertilized crops, and produced on farms that mimic natural ecosystems, and if the meat is eaten in small portions, meat can be an environmentally sustainable food product.

Meat production does not cause global warming because the Earth's warming is natural and not the product of greenhouse gas emissions from livestock or other human-generated sources. Instead, beef and other meat producers offer many benefits: they provide a healthy, nutrient-rich food product for Americans, contribute to the U.S. economy through exports, and help to manage the land through responsible grazing practices.

Chapter 4: What Is the Future for Vegetarianism?

Vegetarianism has grown increasingly acceptable since the 1960s and 1970s, when vegetarian diets first became popular in the United States but were considered a fringe idea. Today, vegetarians are much more respected, and vegetarian foods are widely available. Several prominent members of the vegetarian community sound off on the future of vegetarianism.

Taxes have been useful in reducing the use of tobacco and other known health hazards, but there are even stronger reasons to place a tax on meat. Not only does meat increase the risk of heart disease and colon cancer, it also promotes cruelty towards farm animals, wastes vast quantities of grains and soybeans, uses too much of the world's croplands for animal feed, creates environmental pollution, and is a major contributor to climate change.

Foreword

By definition, controversies are "discussions of questions in which opposing opinions clash" (Webster's Twentieth Century Dictionary Unabridged). Few would deny that controversies are a pervasive part of the human condition and exist on virtually every level of human enterprise. Controversies transpire between individuals and among groups, within nations and between nations. Controversies supply the grist necessary for progress by providing challenges and challengers to the status quo. They also create atmospheres where strife and warfare can flourish. A world without controversies would be a peaceful world; but it also would be, by and large, static and prosaic.

The Series' Purpose

The purpose of the Current Controversies series is to explore many of the social, political, and economic controversies dominating the national and international scenes today. Titles selected for inclusion in the series are highly focused and specific. For example, from the larger category of criminal justice, Current Controversies deals with specific topics such as police brutality, gun control, white collar crime, and others. The debates in Current Controversies also are presented in a useful, timeless fashion. Articles and book excerpts included in each title are selected if they contribute valuable, long-range ideas to the overall debate. And wherever possible, current information is enhanced with historical documents and other relevant materials. Thus, while individual titles are current in focus, every effort is made to ensure that they will not become quickly outdated. Books in the Current Controversies series will remain important resources for librarians, teachers, and students for many years.

In addition to keeping the titles focused and specific, great care is taken in the editorial format of each book in the series. Book introductions and chapter prefaces are offered to provide background material for readers. Chapters are organized around several key questions that are answered with diverse opinions representing all points on the political spectrum. Materials in each chapter include opinions in which authors clearly disagree as well as alternative opinions in which authors may agree on a broader issue but disagree on the possible solutions. In this way, the content of each volume in Current Controversies mirrors the mosaic of opinions encountered in society. Readers will quickly realize that there are many viable answers to these complex issues. By questioning each author's conclusions, students and casual readers can begin to develop the critical thinking skills so important to evaluating opinionated material.

Current Controversies is also ideal for controlled research. Each anthology in the series is composed of primary sources taken from a wide gamut of informational categories including periodicals, newspapers, books, U.S. and foreign government documents, and the publications of private and public organizations. Readers will find factual support for reports, debates, and research papers covering all areas of important issues. In addition, an annotated table of contents, an index, a book and periodical bibliography, and a list of organizations to contact are included in each book to expedite further research.

Perhaps more than ever before in history, people are confronted with diverse and contradictory information. During the Persian Gulf War, for example, the public was not only treated to minute-to-minute coverage of the war, it was also inundated with critiques of the coverage and countless analyses of the factors motivating U.S. involvement. Being able to sort through the plethora of opinions accompanying today's major issues, and to draw one's own conclusions, can be a complicated and frustrating struggle. It is the editors' hope that Current Controversies will help readers with this struggle.

Introduction

> *"Many people think of vegetarianism as a modern phenomena, but various forms of vegetarianism have existed throughout much of human history."*

Vegetarianism is generally defined as a diet that is plant-based and excludes meat. Today, however, there are many different types of vegetarians. Most vegetarians are lacto-ovo-vegetarians who do not eat beef, pork, poultry, fish, shellfish, or animal flesh of any kind, but they do consume both eggs and dairy products. Lacto-vegetarians add eggs to the list of excluded foods but consume dairy products. Even stricter vegetarians, called vegans, do not eat meat of any kind and also do not consume eggs, dairy products, or processed foods containing these or other animal-derived ingredients (such as gelatin). Raw vegans, the most extreme type of vegetarian, believe that cooking food destroys nutrients; they only eat unprocessed vegan foods that have not been heated above 115 degrees Fahrenheit (46 degrees Celsius). At the other end of the spectrum are flextarians—people who eat mostly vegetarian foods but also occasionally eat meat. Many people think of vegetarianism as a modern phenomena, but various forms of vegetarianism have existed throughout much of human history.

For example, despite the stereotype of early man as a fierce hunter of animals for their food, many scientists believe that most human ancestors were actually hunter-gatherers, who primarily ate nuts, seeds, fruits, and vegetables, occasionally supplemented by meat. Scholar and author Jared Diamond, for example, has described going on a hunt with a tribe in New Guinea that uses Stone Age technology to collect two baby birds, a few frogs, and a lot of mushrooms. Exceptions, such as Neanderthal Man—one type of early human who lived in icy parts of what is now northern Europe—are believed to have eaten mostly meat.

The earliest writings about vegetarian diets come from ancient Greece and India. The rise of vegetarianism in India dates to the end of the 6th century BC, when religions such as Buddhism and Jainism first developed. These religions preached the principle of ahimsa, or non-violence, which forbade the killing of animals for religious sacrifice or for meat. These religions spread quickly and soon many people in India embraced vegetarian diets. Vegetarianism continues to be widespread in India today, both for religious and practical reasons. In fact, Indian vegetarians make up about 70 percent of all vegetarians around the globe.

In Greece, the vegetarian trend began about the same time it flourished in India—during the 6th century—with the Greek philosopher Pythagoras. Pythagoras, like the Buddhists, adopted a vegetarian diet for ethical reasons. He and his followers believed that both humans and animals have souls of equal worth, and that animals could be reincarnated as humans and vice versa, so animals should never be killed or eaten. Pythagorians therefore avoided eating meat or eggs and abstained from the traditional animal sacrifices to the Gods. In later decades and centuries, the Pythagorean diet, as it was known, was accepted by many other Greeks, including the famous philosopher Plato. The idea of vegetarianism also survived into Roman times. The Roman poet Ovid and the philosopher Seneca, for example, both promoted the benefits of a vegetarian diet, and scholarly studies suggest that even Roman soldiers mostly ate grains, such as wheat, barley, oats, spelt, and rye, although they also ate some meat.

The fall of Rome and the spread of Christianity throughout Europe, however, resulted in a new form of religious ethics and diet. Christian leaders such as Saint Augustine and Saint Thomas Aquinas argued that only humans have souls and that God gave humans dominion over the natural world, including animals. According to dominant Christian theology, therefore, it became permissible for humans to kill, eat, and otherwise exploit animals. This view continued throughout the Dark Ages in Europe and is accepted by the majority of Christians even today. Only a few orders of monks, such as the Benedictines, Trappists, and Cistercians, practiced vegetarianism during medieval times.

Vegetarianism re-emerged during the European Renaissance—the period of cultural, scientific, and political rebirth that began at the end of the Middle Ages. One of the first famous proponents of vegetarianism was the artist and inventor Leonardo da Vinci (1452–1519), who predicted that humans would one day view the murder of animals as similar to the murder of men. English writer Thomas Tryon (1634–1703) and English poet Percy Bysshe Shelley (1792–1822) were also vocal vegetarians.

In later centuries, vegetarian ideas continued to be held by parts of the population. Scholars maintain that the popularity of vegetarianism during the late nineteenth century was greatly aided by the research of the English naturalist Charles Darwin (1809–1882), whose theory of evolution showed that humans evolved from animals, that humans and animals experience similar feelings and emotions, and that they are separated in intellect only by degree. During this period, prominent vegetarians included German publicist and revolutionist Gustav Struve (1805–1870), Russian author Leo Tolstoy (1828–1910), Irish playwright George Bernard Shaw (1856–1950), and Indian political leader Mohandas Gandhi (1869–1948). England was the site of the strongest vegetarian movement. In 1847, members of the Bible Christian Church, established in 1809 by William Cowherd (1763–1816), founded the Vegetarian Society, a group dedicated to the proposition that Christ's teachings of mercy should be extended to animals. This group still exists and is presently known as the Vegetarian Society of the United Kingdom.

The United States, too, was home to an early vegetarian movement. The writings of Thomas Tryon are believed to have influenced the Quakers, a religious group that promoted principles of nonviolence toward both humans and animals, as well as American inventor and politician Benjamin Franklin (1706–1790)(although Franklin later resumed eating meat). In addition, Reverend William Metcalfe (1788–1862), an American pacifist and member of England's Bible Christian Church, preached vegetarianism and in 1850 became one of the founders of the American Vegetarian Society. Similarly, religious leader Ellen G. White (1827–1915) became a vegetarian and helped to found the Seventh-day Adventist Church, which promotes vegetarianism. Vegetarian ideas also spread in other Western countries, and in 1908 the International Vegetarian Union was formed.

Vegetarianism became even more popular in the 1960s and 1970s, when young people in the United States and other parts of the world became active in anti-war, anti-oppression, pro-environment, and pro-health causes. Many young Hippies, as followers of the youth movement were called, adopted vegetarian diets for environmental, ethical, and political reasons. Vegetarians at this time often credited their decision to a book, *Diet for a Small Planet*, written by American Frances Moore Lappé in 1971. The book, which sold over 3 million copies, presented compelling environmental and economic arguments for not eating meat, including the fact that millions of tons of the world's grain was being fed to livestock instead of hungry people. Lappé's book was followed by a rash of other books promoting vegetarian diets and lifestyles, including many vegetarian cookbooks as well as works criticizing factory farming and advocating for animal liberation. Various vegetarian and animal rights groups were also formed, including People for the Ethical Treatment of Animals (PETA), which was founded in 1980.

Today, in the United States and many other countries, the vegetarian movement is rapidly expanding, and vegetarian foods and products are easily found, even in major supermarkets. Based on the results of a 2000 poll, for example, the Vegetarian Resource Group estimates that there are approximately 4.8 million vegetarians in the United States. Increasingly, people are becoming aware of the health benefits of plant-based diets and the cruel treatment of animals on factory farms. The newest vegetarian campaign has focused on the role of the meat industry in producing greenhouse gases that contribute to global warming. The authors of the viewpoints in *Current Controversies: Vegetarianism* discuss these various aspects of vegetarianism, including health benefits, moral considerations, environmental issues, and the future of the vegetarian movement.

CHAPTER 1

Is Vegetarianism Healthy?

Chapter Overview

SixWise.com

SixWise.com is a Web site that provides health, wealth, and safety recommendations culled from the world's leading experts and specialists.

More than 3 percent of U.S. adults are vegetarians, according to a new study, "Vegetarianism in America," by *Vegetarian Times*. Another 10 percent of adults say they largely follow a vegetarian-inclined diet, while over 5 percent say they are "definitely interested" in following a vegetarian diet in the future.

Among the most common reasons for giving up meat (and in a smaller percentage of cases (0.5 percent), all animal products) were health related. Over half (53 percent) of vegetarians said they eat that way to improve their overall health. Other reasons people gave for becoming vegetarian were:

- Animal welfare (54 percent)

- Environmental concerns (47 percent)

- Natural approaches to wellness (39 percent)

- Food-safety concerns (31 percent)

- Weight loss (25 percent)

- Weight maintenance (24 percent)

But while this style of eating certainly has its devotees, it also has its fair share of critics. So, once and for all, what do the experts say about being a vegetarian? Is it a good choice, a bad choice or, perhaps, somewhere in between?

The Plus-Side to Being a Vegetarian

Many experts agree that vegetarian diets are good for you. According to the American Dietetic Association, for instance, "Vegetarian plans tend to result in lower rates of heart disease, high blood pressure, type 2 diabetes and some forms of cancer. Vegetarians also tend to have lower body mass indexes and cholesterol levels."

Meanwhile, according to research studies posted on GoVeg .com:

- Vegetarians are 50 percent less likely to develop heart disease, and they have a 40 percent lower cancer rate of meat-eaters.

- Meat-eaters are nine times more likely to be obese than vegans (who don't eat any animal products) are.

- Vegetarians have stronger immune systems than meat-eaters.

- Vegetarians and vegans live, on average, six to 10 years longer than meat-eaters.

Many experts agree that vegetarian diets are good for you.

Abstaining from meat, experts say, also helps the environment. According to GoVeg, eating one pound of meat emits the same amount of greenhouse gasses as driving an SUV [sport utility vehicle] 40 miles. And in 2006 the United Nations called the meat industry "one of the top two or three most significant contributors to the most serious environmental problems, at every scale from local to global."

GoVeg even quotes Environmental Defense, which says that "if every American skipped one meal of chicken per week and substituted vegetarian foods instead, the carbon dioxide savings would be the same as taking more than a half-million cars off U.S. roads."

Another plus side often given by vegetarian advocates is the humane treatment of animals. Factory farms, which supply much of the United States' meat, are widely known for their inhumane treatment of animals, and as a vegetarian or vegan you don't support that industry (at least to the extent a conventional meat-eater might).

Eating one pound of meat emits the same amount of greenhouse gasses as driving an SUV 40 miles.

The Down-Side to Being a Vegetarian

According to the Weston A. Price Foundation, a vegetarian diet is far from ideal, mostly because it lacks animal fats, which some experts say are necessary for human health.

"Scientific evidence [shows] that humans need animal foods, particularly animal fats, for optimum health," they say.

"The Foundation believes that strict vegetarianism (veganism) is detrimental to human health. Vegetarianism that includes eggs and raw (unpasteurized) dairy products, organic vegetables and fruits, properly prepared whole grains, legumes, and nuts, and excludes unfermented soy products and processed foods, can be a healthy option for some people. However, some people have difficulty assimilating vitamins, minerals, protein, and other factors from plant foods. These individuals may need a higher proportion of nutrients from animal foods to achieve optimum health."

The late Stephen Byrnes, PhD, RNCP [Registered Nutritional Consulting Practitioner], wrote an article in the *Townsend Letter for Doctors & Patients* that dispelled many "myths" about the benefits of vegetarianism. In it he said, "many of the vegetarian claims cannot be substantiated and some are simply false and dangerous. There are benefits to vegetarian diets for certain health conditions, and some people function better on less fat and protein, but, as a practitioner who has dealt with several former vegetarians and vegans (total vegetarians), I know full well the dangerous effects of a diet devoid of healthful animal products."

The article also quotes [anthropolgist] H. Leon Abrams who said, "Humans have always been meat-eaters. The fact that no human society is entirely vegetarian, and those that are almost entirely vegetarian suffer from debilitated conditions of health, seems unequivocally to prove that a plant diet must be supplemented with at least a minimum amount of animal protein to sustain health. Humans are meat-eaters and always have been. Humans are also vegetable eaters and always have been, but plant foods must be supplemented by an ample amount of animal protein to maintain optimal health."

A vegetarian diet is far from ideal, mostly because it lacks animal fats, which some experts say are necessary for human health.

What about all of the saturated fats in animal foods? According to the Weston A. Price Foundation, they're actually good for you. Here they describe the many roles of saturated fats:

"Contrary to the accepted view, which is not scientifically based, saturated fats do not clog arteries or cause heart disease. In fact, the preferred food for the heart is saturated fat; and saturated fats lower a substance called Lp(a), which is a very accurate marker for proneness to heart disease.

Saturated fats play many important roles in the body chemistry. They strengthen the immune system and are involved in inter-cellular communication, which means they protect us against cancer. They help the receptors on our cell membranes work properly, including receptors for insulin, thereby protecting us against diabetes. The lungs cannot function without saturated fats, which is why children given butter and full-fat milk have much less asthma than children given reduced-fat milk and margarine. Saturated fats are also involved in kidney function and hormone production.

Saturated fats are required for the nervous system to function properly, and over half the fat in the brain is saturated. Saturated fats also help suppress inflammation. Finally, saturated animal fats carry the vital fat-soluble vitamins A, D and K2, which we we need in large amounts to be healthy.

Human beings have been consuming saturated fats from animals products, milk products and the tropical oils for thousands of years; it is the advent of modern processed vegetable oil that is associated with the epidemic of modern degenerative disease, not the consumption of saturated fats."

Feeling confused? You're not alone. There's a lot of conflicting information out there when it comes to diet and nutrition. While the experts continue to battle it out over whether vegetarianism is healthy or harmful, you can take comfort in the fact that there is no right diet for everyone. You need to eat a diet that feels right for you, and that is one thing that almost everyone can agree on.

Plant-Based Diets Provide Many Health Benefits

Winston Craig

Winston Craig is a professor of nutrition at Andrews University, a Seventh-day Adventist educational institution located in Berrien Springs, Michigan.

Recently, there has been a renewed interest in vegetarian diets. Today there are countless books, cookbooks, and magazine articles promoting vegetarian diets and providing guidance for those who wish to follow a meatless diet.

A Short Historical Perspective on Vegetarian Diets

In the past, many viewed vegetarianism as strange and faddish but appropriately planned vegetarian diets are now recognized by many, including the American Dietetic Association, as being nutritionally adequate, and providing healthful benefits in the prevention and treatment of chronic diseases (1).

Choosing a nonvegetarian lifestyle has a significant health and medical cost. The total direct medical costs in the United States attributable to meat consumption were estimated to be $30–60 billion a year, based upon the higher prevalence of hypertension, heart disease, cancer, diabetes, gallstones, obesity and food-borne illness among omnivores compared with vegetarians (2).

A large body of scientific literature suggests that the consumption of a diet of whole grains, legumes, vegetables, nuts, and fruits, with the avoidance of meat and high-fat animal products, along with a regular exercise program is consistently associated with lower blood cholesterol levels, lower blood

Winston Craig, "Health Benefits of Vegetarian Diets," Vegetarianism and Vegetarian Nutrition (www.vegetarian-nutrition.info), 2008. Reproduced by permission.

pressure, less obesity and consequently less heart disease, stroke, diabetes, cancer, and mortality (1,3,4). In African-Americans, the frequent consumption of nuts, fruits and green salads was associated with 35–44 percent lower risk of overall mortality (5).

Distinguishing Feature

A vegetarian diet is distinguished from an omnivorous diet by its content of dry beans and lentils. These take the place of meat and fish as the major source of protein. And there are so many different kinds of beans you can choose from—kidney, lima, pinto, cranberry, navy, Great Northern, garbanzo, soy beans, and black-eyed peas. These can be served with rice, added to soups, stews, and salads or a variety of casseroles, and made into different ethnic dishes.

Tofu, or soy bean curd, can be used in dips and spreads, or served with pasta or stir-fried vegetables. Soy protein contains isoflavones, such as genistein and daidzein, that act as phytoestrogens and inhibit tumor growth, lower blood cholesterol levels, decrease the risk of blood clots, and diminish bone loss. These benefits clearly translate into a lower risk of heart disease, stroke, cancer and osteoporosis (6).

People who consume higher amounts of fruits and vegetables have about one-half the risk of cancer.

Cancer Protection

A major report published by the World Cancer Research Fund in 1997 recommended we lower our risk of cancer by choosing predominantly plant-based diets rich in a variety of vegetables and fruits, legumes and minimally processed starchy staple foods, and to limit the intake of grilled, cured and smoked meats and fish. These methods of preparing meat produce polycyclic aromatic hydrocarbons and heterocyclic amines which are carcinogenic (11).

Over 200 studies have revealed that a regular consumption of fruits and vegetables provides significant protection against cancer at many sites. People who consume higher amounts of fruits and vegetables have about one-half the risk of cancer, especially the epithelial cancers (7). The risk of most cancers was 20–50% lower in those with a high versus a low consumption of whole grains (8).

About three dozen plant foods have been identified as possessing cancer-protective properties. These include cruciferous vegetables (broccoli, Brussels sprouts, cabbage, cauliflower), umbelliferous vegetables and herbs (carrots, celery, cilantro, caraway, dill, parsley), other fruits and vegetables (citrus, tomatoes, cucumber, grapes, cantaloupe, berries), beans (soybeans), whole grains (brown rice, oats, whole wheat), flaxseed, many nuts, and various seasoning herbs (garlic, scallions, onions, chives, ginger, turmeric, rosemary, thyme, oregano, sage, and basil) (9).

These foods and herbs contain a host of cancer-protective phytochemicals such as carotenoids, flavonoids, isothiocyanates, isoflavones, ellagic acid, glucarates, curcumins, liminoids, lignans, phenolic acids, phthalides, saponins, phytosterols, sulfide compounds, terpenoids, and tocotrienols. These beneficial compounds alter metabolic pathways and hormonal actions that are associated with the development of cancer, stimulate the immune system, and have antioxidant activity (10).

Regular fruit and vegetable consumption reduces the risk of ischemic heart disease.

Heart Disease

Regular fruit and vegetable consumption reduces the risk of ischemic heart disease [reduced blood supply to the heart]. A recent survey of 47,000 Italians found that persons in the highest tertile [third] of vegetable consumption had a 21 and 11% reduced risk of myocardial infarction and angina, respectively, compared with those in the lowest tertile of vegetable consumption (12).

A British study found that daily consumption of fresh fruit was associated with a 24 percent reduction in mortality from heart disease and a 32 percent reduction in death from cerebrovascular disease, compared with less frequent fruit consumption. Daily consumption of raw salad was associated with a 26 percent reduction in mortality from heart disease (13).

In another study, lifelong vegetarians had a 24 percent lower incidence and lifelong vegans (those who eat no eggs or dairy products) had a 57 percent lower incidence of coronary heart disease compared to meat eaters (14). Healthy volunteers who consumed a vegetarian diet (25% of calories as fat) that was rich in green, leafy vegetables and other low-calorie vegetables (tomatoes, cucumbers, carrots, bell peppers, celery, green beans, etc.), fruits, nuts, sweet corn and peas experienced after two weeks decreases of 25, 33, 20 and 21 percent in total cholesterol, LDL cholesterol, triglycerides, and total/HDL cholesterol ratio, respectively (15).

Various factors exist in fruits and vegetables that provide possible protection against cardiovascular disease. These factors include folic acid, dietary fiber, potassium, magnesium, carotenoids, phytosterols, flavonoids, and other polyphenolic antioxidants. Typically, vegetarian diets are also somewhat lower in saturated fat and cholesterol. Vegetarians typically have lower blood cholesterol levels. Plant diets rich in soluble fiber (such as found in dry beans, oats, carrots, squash, apples, and citrus) are useful for lowering serum cholesterol levels.

The many flavonoids in fruits, vegetables, nuts and whole grains, have extensive biological properties that reduce the risk of heart disease. Flavonoids are among the most potent antioxidants. They protect LDL cholesterol from oxidation; inhibit the formation of blood clots; and have hypolipidemic effects and anti-inflammatory action (16). European studies found that those who had the highest consumption of flavonoids had 60 percent less mortality from heart disease and 70 percent lower risk of stroke than the low flavonoid consumers (17, 18).

The yellow-orange and red carotenoid pigments in fruits and vegetables are powerful antioxidants that can quench free radicals and protect against cholesterol oxidation. Persons with high levels of serum carotenoids have a reduced risk of heart disease. The recent EURAMIC [European Community Multicenter] study found that a high intake of lycopene (the red pigment in tomatoes, pink grapefruit, and watermelon) was associated in men with a 48 percent lower risk of a myocardial infarction compared with a low intake of lycopene. Cholesterol synthesis is suppressed and LDL receptor activity is augmented by the carotenoids beta-carotene and lycopene, similar to that seen with the drug fluvastatin (20).

Berries, Beans and Grains

Anthocyanin pigments, the reddish pigments found in fruits, such as strawberries, cherries, cranberries, raspberries, blueberries, grapes, and black currants, are very effective in scavenging free radicals, inhibiting LDL [bad] cholesterol oxidation and inhibiting platelet aggregation. Various terpenoids in fruits and vegetables, and tocotrienols in nuts and seeds facilitate lower blood cholesterol levels, by inhibiting HMG-CoA reductase (21). Garlic, onions and other members of the *Allium* family, contain a variety of ajoenes, vinyldithiins, and other sulfide compounds that have antithrombotic action and may lower blood cholesterol and triglyceride levels.

A number of studies have shown that legumes lower blood cholesterol levels, improve blood sugar control, and lower triglyceride levels. Since beans are good sources of soluble fiber, vegetable protein, saponins, phytosterols and polyunsaturated fat, consuming a diet rich in legumes will lower risk of heart disease.

In the Nurses' Health Study, the highest consumption of whole grains was associated with about a 35–40% reduction in risk of heart disease, stroke, and type 2 diabetes. In the Adventist Health Study a regular consumption of whole wheat bread was associated with a 40 to 50% reduced risk of fatal and non-fatal heart disease.

The consumption of a generous suppy of whole grains, legumes, nuts, fruits and vegetables provides protection against chronic diseases such as cancer, cardiovascular disease and diabetes.

Nut Studies

Epidemiological studies have consistently reported that frequent nut consumption is associated with a 30–60% reduction in the risk of coronary heart disease (22). A number of clinical trials have demonstrated the effectiveness of diets containing almonds, pecans, peanuts, hazelnuts, pistachios, macadamia nuts, or walnuts to significantly lower LDL cholesterol levels by 7 to 16 percent, without much change in HDL cholesterol and triglyceride levels (22).

While nuts are high in fat, they are naturally low in saturated fat and most are quite rich in monounsaturated fat. Nuts also contain a number of vitamins, minerals and other substances important for cardiovascular health, such as potassium, magnesium, vitamin E, folic acid, copper, and dietary fiber. In addition, most nuts contain phytosterols, tocotrienols, and protective polyphenolics such as ellagic acid and flavonoids (23).

Stroke and Diabetes

Data from two prospective studies supports a protective relationship between fruit and vegetable consumption and risk of ischemic stroke (24). Cruciferous and green leafy vegetables and citrus fruits were the most protective. Data from the NHANES [National Health and Nutrition Examination Survey] study revealed that consuming fruit and vegetables three or more times a day compared with less than once a day was associated with a 27% lower incidence of stroke, a 42% lower stroke mortality, a 27% lower cardiovascular disease mortality, and a 15% lower all-cause mortality (25). In the Adventist Health Study, non-vegetarians had a risk of fatal stroke that was 20–30% higher than the vegetarians. Data from population studies and human trials provide evidence that vegetarian dietary patterns lower blood pressure (26). Lower systolic blood pressures in elderly vegetarians has been reported to be best accounted for by their lower body weight (27). Vegetarians living in northern Mexico were found to have lower body weights, higher potassium and lower sodium intakes, and lower mean blood pressures than non-vegetarians (28).

Higher consumption of nuts (29) and whole grains (30) has been associated with lower rates of diabetes. In a large prospective study, fruit and vegetable intake was found to be inversely associated with the incidence of diabetes, particularly among women (31). Men and women who reported seldom or never eating fruit or green leafy vegetables had higher mean HbA_{1C} levels than those who had more frequent consumption (32). An increased consumption of fruit and vegetables appears to contribute to the prevention of diabetes.

The consumption of a generous supply of whole grains, legumes, nuts, fruits and vegetables provides protection against chronic diseases such as cancer, cardiovascular disease and diabetes. A plant-based diet is rich in its content of health-promoting factors such as the many phytochemicals.

References

1. Craig, WJ, Mangels AR. Position of the American Dietetic Association: Vegetarian Diets. *J Am Diet Assoc* 2009; 109(7):1266–82.

2. Barnard ND, Nicholson A, and Howard JL. The Medical Costs Attributable to Meat Consumption. *Prev Med* 1995; 24:646–55.

3. Snowdon DA, Phillips RL. Does a Vegetarian Diet Reduce the Occurrence of Diabetes? *Am J Publ Health* 1985; 75:507–512.

4. Dwyer JT. Health Aspects of Vegetarian Diets. *Am J Clin Nutr* 1988; 48:712–38.

5. Fraser GE, Sumbureru D, Pribis S, et al. Association Among Health Habits, Risk Factors, and All-cause Mortality in a Black California Population. *Epidemiology* 1997; 8:168–74.

6. Setchell KDR. Phytoestrogens: The Biochemistry, Physiology, and Implications for Human Health of Soy Isoflavones. *Am J Clin Nutr* 1998; 68(suppl):1333S–46S.

7. Steinmetz K, Potter J. Vegetables, Fruit and Cancer, I. Epidemiology. *Cancer Causes Control* 1991; 2(suppl):325–57.

8. Jacobs DR, Marquart L, Slavin J, et al. Whole-grain Intake and Cancer: An Expanded Review and Meta-analysis. *Nutr Cancer* 1998; 30:85–96.

9. Caragay AB. Cancer-preventative Foods and Ingredients. *Food Tech* 1992; 46(4):65–8.

10. Craig WJ. *Nutrition and Wellness. A Vegetarian Way to Better Health*. Golden Harvest Books, Berrien Springs, MI, 1999.

11. World Cancer Research Fund. *Food, Nutrition and the Prevention of Cancer: A Global Perspective*. World Cancer Research Fund/American Institute for Cancer Research, Washington DC, 1997.

12. Kafatos A, Diacatou A, Voukiklaris G, et al. Heart Disease Risk-factor Status and Dietary Changes in the Cretan Population over the Past 30 y: The Seven Countries Study. *Am J Clin Nutr* 1997; 65:1882–6.

13. Key TJA, Thorogood M, Appleby PN, et al. Dietary Habits and Mortality in 11,000 Vegetarians and Health Conscious People: Results of 17-year Follow Up. *BMJ* 1996; 313:775–79.

14. Thorogood M, Carter R, et al. Plasma Lipids and Lipoprotein Cholesterol Concentrations in People with Different Diets in Britain. *Br Med J* 1987; 295:351–3.

15. Jenkins DJA, Popovich D, Kendall C, et al. Effect of a Diet High in Vegetables, Fruit, and Nuts on Serum Lipids. *Metabolism* 1997; 46:530–7.

16. Manach C, Regerat F, Texier O, et al. Bioavailability, Metabolism and Physiological Impact of 4-oxo-flavonoids. *Nutr Res* 1996; 16:517–44.

17. Hertog MGL, Feskens EJM, Hollman PC, et al. Dietary Antioxidant Flavonoids and Risk of Coronary Heart Disease. *Lancet* 1993; 342:1007–11.

18. Keli SO, Hertog MG, Feskins EJ, et al. Dietary Flavonoids, Antioxidant Vitamins, and Incidence of Stroke: The Zutphen Study. *Arch Intern Med* 1996; 156:637–42.

19. Clinton SK. Lycopene: Chemistry, Biology, and Implications for Human Health and Disease. *Nutr Rev* 1998; 56:35–51.

20. Fuhrman B, Elis A, Aviram M. Hypocholesterolemic Effect of Lycopene and Beta-carotene Is Related to Suppression of Cholesterol Synthesis and Augmentation of LDL Receptor Activity in Macrophages. *Biochem Biophys Res Comm* 1997; 233:658–62.

21. Pearce BC, Parker RA, Deason ME, et al. Hypocholesterolemic Activity of Synthetic and Natural Tocotrienols. *J Med Chem* 1992; 35:3595–606.

22. Kris-Etherton PM, Zhao G, Binkoski AE, Coval SM, Etherton TD. The Effects of Nuts on Coronary Heart Disease Risk. *Nutr Rev* 2001 Apr; 59(4):103–11.

23. Dreher ML, Maher CV, Kearney P. The Traditional and Emerging Role of Nuts in Healthful Diets. *Nutr Rev* 1996; 54:241–5.

24. Joshipura KJ, Ascherio A, Manson JF, et al. Fruit and Vegetable Intake in Relation to Risk of Ischemic Stroke. *JAMA* 1999; 282:1233–9.

25. Bazzano LA, He J, Ogden LG, et al. Fruit and Vegetable Intake and Risk of Cardiovascular Disease in US Adults: The First National Health and Nutrition Examination Survey Epidemiologic Follow-up Study. *Am J Clin Nutr* 2002; 76:93–9.

26. Beilin LJ, Burke V. Vegetarian Diet Components, Protein and Blood Pressure: Which Nutrients Are Important? *Clin Exp Pharmacol Physiol* 1995; 22:195–8.

27. Melby CL, Lyle RM, Poehlman ET. Blood Pressure and Body Mass Index in Elderly Long-term Vegetarians and Non-vegetarians. *Nutr Rep Intern* 1988; 37(1):47.

28. Wyatt CJ, Velazquez A, Grijalva C, et al. Dietary Intake of Sodium, Potassium and Blood Pressure in Lacto-ovo-vegetarians. *Nutr Res* 1995; 15:819–30.

29. Jiang R, Manson JE, Stampfer MJ, et al. Nut and Peanut Butter Consumption and Risk of Type 2 Diabetes in Women. *JAMA* 2002; 288:2554–60.

30. Fung TT, Hu FB, Pereira MA, et al. Whole-grain Intake and the Risk of Type 2 Diabetes: A Prospective Study in Men. *Am J Clin Nutr* 2002; 76:535–40.

31. Ford ES, Mokdad AH. Fruit and Vegetable Consumption and Diabetes Mellitus Incidence Among U.S. Adults. *Prev Med* 2001 Jan; 32:33–9.

32. Sargeant LA, Khaw KT, Bingham S, et al. Fruit and Vegetable Intake and Population Glycosylated Haemoglobin Levels: The EPIC-Norfolk Study. *Eur J Clin Nutr* 2001; 55:342–8.

A Strict Vegetarian Diet Is Unhealthy for Most People

Ben Kim

Ben Kim is a chiropractor and acupuncturist living and working in Barrie, Ontario, Canada.

Have you ever watched an animal being butchered? Unless you have experienced it many times, I bet you would feel quite bad watching it, let alone doing it yourself. Watching the butchering of an animal certainly helps people understand the passion that animal rights groups have in promoting a strict vegan (plant-based) diet.

From a moral and ethical perspective, I really appreciate the reasons for being a strict vegan. In fact, if I knew that I could be healthy on such a diet, I believe that I would return to being a strict vegan. The reality is that as far as recorded history is concerned, there has never been a population of people in our world that has lived on a strict vegan diet for an entire lifespan. Some populations have eaten mostly plant foods, but to my knowledge, there has not been a single population that has been on a 100 percent plant-based diet.

Today, there are many organizations that use their books and literature to promote a 100 percent strict vegan diet for optimal health for everyone.

Health Risks of Strict Vegan Diets

Well, my experiences with my own body and in providing health care to many people over the years have led me to believe that a long term, strict vegan diet is likely to lead to the development of nutritional deficiencies and significant health problems for most people. Whenever I have shared this view with people who are just getting started with and excited about a strict vegan diet, I am usually asked to consider specific people or communities that claim to thrive on a strict vegan diet, some for decades.

I believe that people can survive for many years on a strict vegan diet, but almost always with one or more significant health problems. And I believe that some people who are truly thriving without any health problems, and claim to have been strict vegans for many years usually eat some animal foods, even if it is a small amount. The fact is, you and I can never know with certainty what another person eats on a moment-to-moment basis. The only dietary regimen that you can know with absolute accuracy is your own. Even your dog or cat probably eats things that you don't know about.

A long term, strict vegan diet is likely to lead to the development of nutritional deficiencies and significant health problems for most people.

The Failings of Pro-Vegan Organizations

Getting back to the organizations that promote vegan diets, I had the opportunity a short while ago to spend several days with a person who used to work for one of them. This person told me that their organization's recommendation to eat a strict vegan diet is mainly to support their mission of preventing cruel treatment of animals. My guess is that organizations like this are well aware that more people will be persuaded to follow a strict vegan diet if they believe it is for their health than if it's for the welfare of animals.

I respect animal rights groups that come right out and say that they are promoting a strict vegan diet for the welfare of animals. If you are going to choose to be a strict vegan to spare animals pain, even if this means that your health might suffer, I can respect your decision.

But let's not confuse compassion for animals with striving to do what's best for your health.

I believe that people who choose to be strict vegans for the welfare of animals need to consider this question: is promoting a 100 percent vegan diet for the welfare of animals a correct moral path if it leads to significant health problems for humans? Personally, I feel bad about an animal being killed to be my food. But if there were no fishermen or farmers around, I believe that I would gratefully sacrifice an animal with my own hands since I believe that the health of my family requires eating small amounts of animal foods.

What about organizations that promote a 100 percent vegan diet strictly for health reasons? I think that these organizations can thrive because many people who first make the conversion from a highly processed and animal-based diet to a strict vegan diet typically experience incredible improvement with their health. For a few months or even a year or two, many people can thrive on a strict vegan diet, making it easy for them to believe that they have discovered a diet that will best support their health for the rest of their lives. But then, as most of them predictably become deficient in nutrients that are difficult to obtain from plant foods alone, they usually become confused about why their health is suffering.

This is where I believe these organizations fail and even contribute to worsening of health. Rather than consider each person as being unique and having unique requirements for health, in my view, they seem more interested in trying to fit everyone into their programs and philosophies. Health problems that people experience while on their programs are often attributed to detoxification or a period of adaptation. Sometimes, the reason given for why you aren't doing well with their programs is that your spiritual or emotional health is suffering. Now, I completely agree that your spiritual and emotional health have significant impact on your overall health, but I really hope that you remain open to tinkering with all areas of your life—including what you eat—when looking to get healthier.

Do I believe that some of these groups know that a strict vegan diet is not healthy for everyone in the long term but continue to promote it to their followers? I cannot say for sure. But I will say that I believe that the decision to stick to recommending a strict vegan diet for the long term is often for business reasons or because of an interest in protecting animals than it is about honestly observing what's working and what's not.

Eating lots of plant-based foods is good for your health. Eating ONLY plant-based foods for the long term is not likely to be good for your health.

Trusting Your Body

Please know that I'm not asking you to blindly believe my opinion about a long term, strict vegan diet being unhealthy for most people in the long term. I'm encouraging you to be honest with yourself about how you feel. If you have been a strict vegan for more than a year and have noticed problems like feeling tired a lot, not sleeping well, weak hair and nails, sensitive and decaying teeth, inability to maintain a healthy weight, constant hunger, unexplained irritability, or depression, isn't it worth your while to at least consider that your diet isn't working for you? How long are you supposed to attribute these and other health problems to detoxification or a period of adjustment?

If you are a strict vegan eating mainly whole, unprocessed plant foods, and you are experiencing health challenges, you can probably experience dramatically better health just by adding some organic eggs to your diet. Organic eggs from free range birds and organic butter are two foods that will provide you with essential nutrients that are not abundant or present at all in plant foods and may not conflict with your compassion for animals.

In fact, my experiences have led me to believe that many people don't need to get more than 10–25 percent of their total calories from clean, organic animal foods to be at their best. Just in the past year alone, I have worked with several people who were experiencing significant health challenges on a long term, strict vegan diet and were extremely grateful to see their health improve by adding small amounts of clean animal foods to their diets.

Here's my final take on this topic: eating lots of plant-based foods is good for your health. Eating ONLY plant-based foods for the long term is not likely to be good for your health.

But don't blindly trust me or anyone else on this important topic.

Trust your own body.

A Vegetarian Diet Can Be Hazardous if It's Not Nutritionally Balanced

Victoria Anisman-Reiner

Victoria Anisman-Reiner is a writer, a teacher in holistic health and energy healing, and an aromatherapist.

Vegetarianism has benefits that are both global and health-related. But those who think vegetarianism is an easy, worry-free way to achieve better health would do well to consider some of the long-term implications of not eating meat, or, for vegans, any animal products. The challenges include getting enough protein and B vitamins in your diet, as well as ensuring that you don't go overboard on soy, processed foods, unhealthy sugars and carbs. A vegetarian diet can be full of unexpected pitfalls if you're not prepared to work on getting balanced nutrition.

Challenges of Vegetarianism

Finding a good source of protein for each meal can be a challenge, at first, for vegetarians. Most North Americans are accustomed to having some form of meat at each meal, even when another high-protein food is present, yet for vegetarians it is these other sources of essential amino acids that are vital for a balanced diet. Without adequate amounts of each of the 9 essential amino acids, some vegetarians experience "brain fog," memory loss, tiredness, moodiness due to blood sugar highs and lows, lack of motivation, and poor performance at work or during exercise. Westerners living in enough relative wealth to contemplate vegetarianism as a lifestyle choice will

Victoria Anisman-Reiner, "Disadvantages of Going Veg: A Guide to those Considering the Health Impact of Vegetarianism," *Suite 101: Holistic Nutrition*, February 12, 2007. Reproduced by permission of the author.

almost never experience the kind of protein starvation that results in serious illnesses—but even slight protein deficiency can have a real impact on mental and physical health.

Most vegetarians and particularly vegans must supplement their B vitamins, calcium, and iron or eat fortified foods like protein bars/powders, soy or rice milk, and cereals.

Similarly, vitamin B, iron, calcium, and other vitamins and minerals are a concern for vegans and vegetarians. Meat, eggs, and dairy are generally considered the best sources for these nutrients, some of which—such as B12—cannot be readily absorbed or processed in the human body from plant sources (B12 is the most common nutritional deficiency in the developing world and possibly in the US, reports the *Harvard Health Letter*). For this reason most vegetarians and particularly vegans must supplement their B vitamins, calcium, and iron or eat fortified foods like protein bars/powders, soy or rice milk, and cereals (which are, to varying degree, processed in ways that may be unhealthy).

Iron and calcium are especially a concern for vegetarian women, who have to make up the iron lost monthly as blood hemoglobin during their period, and are more at risk than men of developing osteoporosis if their body's calcium needs are not sufficiently met.

If you are vegetarian and your body's need for protein, key vitamins, or minerals is not being met, one of the first warning signals may be a lack of energy—but a deficiency that makes one person feel listless and fatigued may have no effect on another. The amount of protein and vitamins needed can be highly individual. For this reason, it can be helpful to do some of your own research and discuss these issues with an expert nutritionist on vegan and vegetarian diets.

Unhealthy Vegetarian Foods

One of the reasons that many health professionals consider a vegetarian diet unhealthy is the routine dependence on carbohydrates to fill the gap left by meat and other animal-based foods. Younger vegetarians are especially likely to lean on bread, cereal grains, sugary fruits, and desserts to fill them up while the rest of their family is eating meat or poultry, but adult vegetarians can fall prey to carbohydrate dependency and addiction as well. Foods rich in protein take longer for the body to digest and will fill you up, so a meal without enough protein will naturally leave a person hungry and can lead to overeating—usually of carbs. Excessive carbs and sugars becomes a vicious cycle, since eating sugar tends to make you crave more sweets. An unbalanced vegetarian diet without sufficient protein can lead to sugar addiction, blood sugar highs and lows, and in the long term even diabetes.

Many health professionals consider a vegetarian diet unhealthy . . . [because of] the routine dependence on carbohydrates to fill the gap left by meat and other animal-based foods.

Other unhealthy vegetarian foods to watch out for include margarine (made of highly processed hydrogenated or partially hydrogenated fats; even "soft" non-hydrogenated margarine often contains toxic additives) and soy—which can be healthy in moderation, but dubious in large quantities since it can create hormone imbalances in both men and women. Heavily processed veg protein foods like textured soy protein, seitan, and fake meats (veggie dogs, veggie "chicken," "tofurkey," veggie slices) are good in extreme moderation but are very difficult for most people to digest because of their additives and the degree of processing they undergo.

Fortified rice/soy drinks and other foods that vegetarians are often directed towards can also be a mixed blessing. The sources of the vitamins and minerals in these foods are rarely listed and may be from natural or, more usually, from cheap manufactured sources that are difficult for the body to absorb and make use of—so you receive hardly any useable nutrition from them.

A vegetarian diet is, by definition, neither healthy nor unhealthy—like any diet, it depends on the extent of your knowledge and how much care you take to eat foods in balance, get the right nutrition for your body, and avoid overly processed foods and sugars. The website for VIVA, Vegetarians International Voice for Animals, summarizes nicely: "The truth is, most people who eat meat don't give a second thought to diet and nutrition and that's one of the reasons that diet-related illnesses such as obesity, diabetes and many cancers are on the increase." Vegetarianism comes with its own set of associated risks, but if you care enough to be a vegetarian, it's in your interest to give a second thought to your diet, take the time to get it right and do what's best for your health.

A Vegetarian Diet Is Healthy for Teenagers

Center for Young Women's Health

Center for Young Women's Health is an educational organization operated by Children's Hospital Boston that provides teen girls and young women with carefully researched health information and education.

A vegetarian is someone who does not eat meat, including beef, chicken, pork, or fish. Some vegetarians may or may not choose to eat animal products such as eggs, milk, gelatin, or honey. There are different types of vegetarians:

- *Lacto-ovo vegetarian*
  Lacto-ovo vegetarians do not eat meat but do eat eggs and dairy products (ovo means eggs and lacto means dairy).

- *Lacto vegetarian*
  Lacto vegetarians do not eat meat but do eat dairy products.

- *Ovo vegetarian*
  Ovo vegetarians do not eat meat but do eat eggs.

- *Vegan*
  Vegans avoid eating any animal products. Vegans do not eat any meat products, milk, cheese, eggs, honey, or gelatin. Many vegans choose not to wear clothes containing animal products, such as leather, wool, or silk, or wear makeup tested on animals.

Center for Young Women's Health, "How to Be a Healthy Vegetarian: A Guide for Teens," February 5, 2009. Copyright © 2010 Center for Young Women's Health, Children's Hospital Boston. All rights reserved. Used with permission. www.young womenshealth.org.

Why Do People Decide to Be Vegetarian?

People decide to become a vegetarian for many reasons. Some common motivators include the environment, animal rights, and health. You may have different reasons. Deciding to become vegetarian is an individual decision.

Eating a balanced diet when you are vegetarian usually requires a little extra attention.

Are Vegetarian Diets Healthy?

Vegetarian diets can be very healthy, but eating a balanced diet when you are vegetarian usually requires a little extra attention. Because vegetarians eliminate certain foods from their diets, they often need to work to add foods into their diet that will provide the nutrients found in meat products. By eating a variety of foods including fruits, vegetables, and whole grains, you can get nutrients you need from non-meat sources. Vegans need to pay special attention to getting enough iron, calcium, vitamin D, and vitamin B12.

- Carbohydrates provide energy and vitamins for your brain and muscles. Grain products, especially whole grains, are very important because they provide the carbohydrate, fiber, and many vitamins that your body needs.

- Fat is needed by your body to stay healthy. Fat provides essential fatty acids and helps your body absorb certain vitamins. Vegetarians need to include sources of fat such as nuts, oils, or avocado.

- Protein is needed for your muscles to grow. Vegetarians have to be careful not to just cut meat out of their diet, but to replace the meat with high-protein vegetarian foods. Nuts, peanut butter, soy foods, and legumes such as beans, peas, and lentils all provide protein. Protein is also found in dairy foods such as milk, yogurt, and cheese for vegetarians who eat these foods.

- Zinc is important for growth and your immune system. Zinc is found in whole grains, fortified breakfast cereals, dairy products, soy foods, and legumes.

- Iron is important for your blood and is found in beans, seeds, soy foods, fortified breakfast cereals, and dark green leafy vegetables, like spinach. Vitamin C helps your body to absorb iron so it is important to eat foods rich in vitamin C, such as citrus fruits and certain vegetables (such as tomatoes) as well.

- Calcium is required to build strong bones for later in life. Calcium is found in dairy products such as milk, yogurt and cheese. Some foods are not naturally high in calcium but have calcium added to them; these foods are called calcium-fortified. Some soy products, orange juices, cereals, and cereal bars are calcium fortified. Look at the Nutrition Facts Label to find out which brands are highest in calcium.

- Vitamin D is necessary for strong bones and is particularly important for people who live in colder climates because you need the sun to make it. During the winter the sun is not as strong and you are not able to make enough vitamin D. Therefore, it is especially important to make sure you get vitamin D from the foods you eat, such as fortified dairy products and soy milk, or from a supplement.

- Vitamin B_{12} is only found in animal foods, so vegans must eat food fortified with B_{12}. Examples include nutritional yeast flakes, fortified soymilk, and fortified cereals.

A Vegan Diet Can Cause Malnourishment, Especially in Children

Natasha Mann

Natasha Mann is a journalist from the United Kingdom whose articles have appeared in The Independent, The Scotsman, *and other U.K. newspapers.*

One morning over breakfast, Holly Paige looked at her daughter and realised things weren't right. Lizzie should have been flourishing. Instead, her cheeks were pinched, she was small for her age, and although she had skinny arms and legs, her belly was big and swollen. When Lizzie smiled, Paige suddenly noticed her upper front teeth were pitted with holes.

"I was absolutely horrified," recalls Paige.

At the time, Paige was feeding them what she thought was the most nutritious diet possible. They had been raw vegans for three years, and ate plenty of fruit, vegetables, nuts, seeds, grains, soya and pulses, but no meat, fish or dairy. According to the raw-food doctrine, Lizzie and Bertie, then three and four-and-a-half, should have been brimming with good health. But Paige's mothering instinct was on the alert.

"I knew something was wrong, but I couldn't put a finger on it," says Paige, 45. "They were two sizes behind in clothes. Of course, children come in all different shapes and sizes, but their growth seemed to be slowing further. I have two older children so I had their development to measure Lizzie and Bertie's against."

There were other oddities: "I remember going to the supermarket and buying butter for my older children. Lizzie, who had never had butter in her life, would grab the packet and gnaw into it," says Paige. "It was really disconcerting. I would be thinking, 'What is going on? Here is this purely fed child—why would she need to do this?' I was so brainwashed into thinking dairy products are bad for you."

When she took Lizzie and Bertie to her health visitor, she didn't seem too concerned. "She said they were in the low percentile, but thought they were OK," says Paige. "Yet I knew the children weren't growing. I could sense that there was something wrong. It felt wrong."

Finally, Paige stumbled across the answer in an old vitamin book. Although she has no medical confirmation, she believes the family had symptoms of vitamin D- and protein-deficiency. "I felt like such an idiot. I got the information from a book I'd had sitting around on my shelf for 20 years."

The discovery brought a swift end to her experience of veganism. In Totnes [United Kingdom], where she lives, Paige knows many other raw vegans who have a nature-loving lifestyle. But despite taking a daily supplement that included vitamin D and B12, she and the children were suffering. Today, the family still mainly has a raw diet, but Paige includes butter, cheese, eggs and occasionally fish. "I had let malnutrition in through the back door in the name of health," says Paige. "It was ridiculous."

Many dieticians believe it is possible to bring up a healthy vegan child [but] . . . "you do have to make sure you know what you are doing."

Dangers of a Vegan Diet

There is a significant difference between being vegan (and eating cooked foods) and raw vegan. Vegans benefit from fortified cereals, baked goods and a wider variety of grains and pulses; what's more, cooking aids the absorption of some micronutrients. But Lisa Miles, from the British Nutrition Foundation, says: "The most dramatic change to the diet is being vegan rather than the raw element, because you are cutting out two huge food groups. This affects vitamin D and protein."

Last week [June 2008], strict diets for children were questioned after a 12-year-old vegan girl was admitted to a Scottish hospital with rickets. Her spine was said to resemble that of an 80-year-old woman.

Rickets is a degenerative bone condition that can lead to curvature of the spine and bone fractures. It is caused by a lack of vitamin D, usually found in oily fish, eggs, butter and made by our bodies from sunshine—although in the UK [United Kingdom] the sun is only strong enough to do this between April and September. It's a disease you might more commonly associate with the Dickensian character, Tiny Tim.

Several factors ... make a vegan diet for small children more difficult.

Many dieticians believe it is possible to bring up a healthy vegan child. "You can do it, but you do have to make sure you know what you are doing, especially in regards to weight," says Jackie Lowdon from the British Dietician Association. "As with any self-restricting diet, you need to get proper professional advice."

The Vegan Society, unsurprisingly, claim that the diet is suitable for all stages of life, and have an army of strapping, healthy adults brought up as vegans from birth who are happy to talk to the media. They also publish a book with dietary advice on feeding vegan children, written by dietician Sandra Hood. A spokeswoman, however, says they would not recommend a raw vegan diet for children.

Nigel Denby, a dietician and author of *Nutrition for Dummies*, says: "It can be hard enough bringing a child up to eat healthily, but with a vegan diet you are really making a difficult job for yourself. It is absolutely not something that should be tried without support from a dietician."

Several factors, says Denby, make a vegan diet for small children more difficult. With a restricted range of foods, if children turn their nose up at one particular food, you could be stuck for choice. "With smaller appetites and portion sizes, children under five have higher nutrient requirements than adults. Therefore, every mealtime has to be an opportunity to feed them high-nutrient-based foods."

Care must be taken with certain nutrients. "Haem iron, found in meat, is easier for the body to absorb," explains Denby. "Non-haem iron, which is just as good, is found in leafy vegetables and fortified cereals, but you have to eat a greater amount to get the same amount of iron."

Paige now believes that her children were craving dairy products. "It was confusing because for the first year I felt good, calm and content, and had plenty of energy. The children didn't have childhood sicknesses. But something seemed to be missing. We were always picking between meals, always obsessed by food."

Paige believes long-term breastfeeding helped sustain Lizzie and Bertie, but the toll of veganism on her own health was dramatic: "It was the third year when my body started disintegrating, frighteningly fast. I was getting thin, losing muscle and I was going to bed at half nine." She would also have "mad" binges, and eat nothing but rice cakes and butter.

Experience shows a lot of us can't get enough protein on a vegan diet.

The last straw came when Paige's eldest son Bruce came to stay. He asked her to buy chicken, and Paige ended up eating half of it. After that, she couldn't stop. "I just went wild. Typically, in a day I would eat half a chicken, two litres of milk, half a pound of cheese and three eggs. I just had to do it. It went on for weeks. The children were having lots of boiled eggs and cheese."

Paige, who now runs an online magazine and raw food shop, says her biggest lesson is never to be too restrictive again. "For a lot of people, there is something about these various nutrients in the animal form that we can assimilate. I don't know why, but experience shows a lot of us can't get enough protein on a vegan diet."

Now when Paige looks at her two youngest, now seven and eight, she is certain they are thriving. "There was a moment when I was worried damage had been done for life," she says. "Now, I'm confident they are doing well. Even though they eat as much fruit and dried fruit as before, their teeth haven't had one bit more decay."

And nowadays, it's their growth that's the big talking point. "The first thing anyone says when they visit is: 'My, haven't they grown?'"

Nutrients That Everyone Needs

B12

Because this vitamin is mainly found in meat, dairy products and eggs, vegans must get it from other sources such as supplements, fortified breakfast cereals and Marmite. Deficiency can lead to irreversible nervous system damage.

Vitamin D

Our skins make vitamin D when exposed to the sun's ultraviolet rays. But with desk-bound jobs, long winters and unpredictable weather, it is not always possible to get enough. Vitamin D is crucial for bone growth in children, and deficiency can result in rickets. Oily fish is one of the best dietary sources, but vegans can obtain it from fortified breakfast cereals and margarine. People living in Scotland may need to take greater care over vitamin D, as may people from cultures that require them to cover up.

Calcium

Found in dairy products, this is essential for strong bones. It is often lacking in a vegan diet unless taken as a supplement.

Iron

Without sufficient iron, vegans and vegetarians can become anaemic. Deficiency can also delay growth in toddlers. Iron is commonly found in meat, but vegetarians can source iron from pulses and leafy green vegetables.

Calories

Although childhood obesity is an issue today, not enough calories can mean children don't grow properly. This can be a problem in high-fibre diets.

Protein

High-biological-value protein is found in meat, fish, eggs and dairy products. Low-biological-value protein is found in nuts, pulses and wholegrains. Separately, the latter don't contain all the essential amino acids, but do when combined correctly. Knowledge of which foods to mix together is therefore crucial.

Young Vegetarians May Be at Increased Risk of Eating Disorders

Sylvia Byrd and Daphne Pierce-Smith

Sylvia Byrd and Daphne Pierce-Smith are registered nurses and online medical reviewers for the Web site of Frye Regional Medical Center, a private medical facility in Hickory, North Carolina.

Despite its proven health benefits, a vegetarian diet might in fact be masking an underlying eating disorder, new research suggests.

The study, in the April issue of the *Journal of the American Dietetic Association*, found that twice as many teens and nearly double the number of young adults who had been vegetarians reported having used unhealthy means to control their weight, compared with those who had never been vegetarians. Those means included using diet pills, laxatives and diuretics and inducing vomiting to control weight.

The Dark Side of Vegetarianism

There's a dark side to vegetarianism, said Dr. David L. Katz, director of the Prevention Research Center at Yale University School of Medicine. He had no role in the research.

"Adolescent vegetarians [in the study] were more prone to disordered eating and outright eating disorders," Katz said. "This is not due to vegetarianism but the other way around: Adolescents struggling to control their diets and weight might opt for vegetarianism among other, less-healthful efforts."

Vegetarianism, or a mostly plant-based diet, can be recommended to all adolescents, Katz said. "But when adolescents opt for vegetarianism on their own, it is important to find out why because it may signal a cry for help, rather than the pursuit of health," he said.

Katz said he thinks a balanced vegetarian diet is among the most healthful of dietary patterns, and the study suggests some of the benefits.

"Adolescents practicing vegetarianism were less likely to be overweight than their omnivorous counterparts and, were the measures available, would likely have had better blood pressure and cholesterol, too" he said. "Eating mostly plants—and even only plants—is good for us, and certainly far better for health than the typical American diet."

The study's lead researcher, Ramona Robinson-O'Brien, an assistant professor in the Nutrition Department at the College of Saint Benedict and Saint John's University in St. Joseph, Minn., agreed.

There's a dark side to vegetarianism.

"The majority of adolescents and young adults today would benefit from improvements in dietary intake," she said. The study found, for instance, that the vegetarians among the participants generally were less likely to be overweight or obese.

"However, current vegetarians may be at increased risk for binge eating, while former vegetarians may be at increased risk for extreme unhealthful weight-control behaviors," she said. "Clinicians and nutrition professionals providing guidance to young vegetarians might consider the potential benefits associated with a healthful vegetarian diet, [but should] recognize the possibility of increased risk of disordered eating behaviors."

The Study

The researchers collected data on 2,516 teens and young adults who participated in a study called Project EAT-II: Eating

Among Teens. They classified participants as current, former or never vegetarians and divided them into two age groups: teens (15 to 18) and young adults (19–23).

Each participant was questioned about binge eating, whether they felt a loss of control of their eating habits and whether they used any extreme weight-control behaviors.

About 21 percent of teens who had been vegetarians said they used unhealthy weight-control behaviors, compared with 10 percent of teens who had never been vegetarians. Among young adults, more former vegetarians (27 percent) had used such measures than current vegetarians (16 percent) or those who'd never been vegetarians (15 percent), the study found.

In addition, among teenagers, binge eating and loss of control over eating habits was reported by 21 percent of current and 16 percent of former vegetarians but only 4 percent of those who'd never followed a vegetarian diet. For young adults, more vegetarians (18 percent) said they engaged in binge eating with loss of control than did former vegetarians (9 percent) and those who were never vegetarians (5 percent), the study found.

Young adult vegetarians were less likely to be overweight or obese than were those who'd never been vegetarians. Among teens, the study found no statistically significant differences in weight.

"When guiding adolescent and young adult vegetarians in proper nutrition and meal planning, it is important to recognize the potential health benefits and risks associated with a vegetarian diet," Robinson-O'Brien said. "Furthermore, it may be beneficial to investigate an individual's motives for choosing a vegetarian diet and ask about their current and former vegetarian status when assessing risk for disordered eating behaviors."

CHAPTER 2

Is Vegetarianism Morally Superior to a Meat Diet?

Chapter Preface

The bucolic image of cows and other farm animals being raised in peaceful, green pastures by small farmers is no longer the reality of the vast majority of U.S. or global meat production. Over the last 50 years, the way food animals are produced has changed drastically, from a network of small and medium-sized family farms to a system of large, corporate-owned industrial operations, often called factory farms. In fact, according the research group Worldwatch Institute, 74 percent of the world's poultry, 68 percent of eggs, 50 percent of pork, and 43 percent of beef is now produced by factory farms. This transformation of the meat industry is the product of advancements in farm equipment, grain production, transportation, refrigeration, antibiotics, and other technologies that dramatically increased meat production efficiencies, allowing more meat to be produced at more affordable prices.

The first development that paved the way for industrial meat production was the mechanization of agriculture in the mid-1800s. Beginning with Cyrus McCormick's invention of the reaper in 1831, virtually every aspect of farming became mechanized as mechanical planters, huskers, manure spreaders, and other farm equipment were invented to reduce the labor required for farming. During this same period, improvements in transportation and food preservation helped farmers deliver their produce to market. New railroads were built connecting Midwestern farm regions with rapidly growing cities in the eastern United States, and new refrigeration technologies allowed for year-round transport of fresh and frozen plant and meat products.

Following World War II, farming became more commercialized when chemical manufacturers previously involved in the war effort began producing pesticides, herbicides, and synthetic fertilizers for American farmers. U.S. farm policies encouraged farmers to embrace these new products and provided farm subsidies—monies paid to farmers who grow various commodity crops, such as wheat and corn. These technologies and policies helped to produce the Green Revolution—a worldwide increase in agricultural production from about 1940 through the 1960s that helped to feed the Earth's rapidly growing population. The Green Revolution, in fact, produced such an abundance of inexpensive corn and other grains that these crops could also be used to feed animals. The result was that livestock that used to be grass-fed and pasture-raised could now be fed and raised more intensively, making larger-scale animal agriculture operations possible.

Advances in genetic selection and new technologies in farm animal management also contributed to the emerging industrial model of meat production. Increasingly, farm animals were genetically programmed to produce more meat product; housed in large numbers in indoor facilities for ease of handling; fed special foods, hormones, and supplements designed to make them grow or produce quickly; and given antibiotics to prevent disease. These changes have helped, since 1960, to double milk production, triple meat production, and increase egg production fourfold. Meat is also produced much faster. A recent report states that it now takes just forty-five days to produce a five-pound chicken, compared with eighty-four days in 1950.

Today, these animal factory farms, called industrial farm animal production (IFAP) systems or confined animal feeding operations (CAFOs), raise thousands of animals from just a few species in crowded conditions in large buildings. Although there are some laws and guidelines governing how animals should be housed or slaughtered, animals in factory farms are generally treated as production units with little regard to their comfort or needs. Meat production has also become more integrated, with all phases of animal production and processing owned by the same company, and more consolidated, with just a few large corporations dominating the industry. For example, in 2005, four companies controlled over 80 percent of U.S. beef production and processing; three of these same four companies (along with an additional fourth) process over 60 percent of the country's pork; and four major companies provide over half of the country's chicken supply. This American model of farming has also been adopted by other developed countries.

The gains in efficiency and production made by factory farms, however, have come at great cost to both farm animals and the environment. Animal rights critics claim that many standard factory farm practices cause production animals to live lives of constant pain, suffering, and abuse. Most farm animals today live out their lives in tiny cages surrounded by metal bars or packed into enormous windowless buildings. They often are kept in the dark, never seeing the light of day. They are given virtually no space to move around; subjected to horrible mutilations, such as beak searing, tail docking, ear cutting, and castration; and sometimes slaughtered while they are still alive.

In addition, environmentalists argue that the factory farm system hurts the environment and is unsustainable. Large animal production facilities require massive amounts of land and water resources and produce air and water pollution due to the huge amounts of animal waste. In addition, the overuse of antibiotics in these facilities has contributed to a growing problem of antibiotic resistance, affecting human health. Factory farms also contribute significantly to global warming, both because it takes large amounts of fossil fuels to produce animal feed and because so many animals produce large amounts of methane, one of the most potent greenhouse gases. As a recent report by the Pew Commission on Industrial Farm Animal Production has pointed out, these health and environmental impacts loom even larger in the future, because of the growing world population, the rapid economic development in countries such as India and China, and an exploding global demand for meat and poultry. Because of this demand, the factory farming model is now being adopted by newly developing countries—a trend that could bring even greater environmental degradation.

This dark side of animal factory farms, for many people, raises questions about whether it is ethical to eat meat. The authors of the viewpoints included in this chapter discuss whether vegetarianism is morally superior to a meat diet.

Vegetarians Can Claim the Moral High Ground

Riva Gold

Riva Gold is a columnist for the McGill Tribune, *a newspaper published by the Students' Society of McGill University, a college in Quebec, Canada.*

I'm not a zealot, an animal liberationist, or dedicated to the pursuit of global misery. But I've been a vegetarian for nine years—for moral reasons. I don't claim to live among intolerant, meat-eating hooligans who throw cooked flesh into my mouth when I'm not looking in order to relieve me of the disease that is vegetarianism. However, I don't understand why meat eaters don't concede the moral high ground to us.

I agree wholeheartedly with [*McGill Tribune* columnist] Eric Weiss when, in his last column, he described People for the Ethical Treatment of Animals [PETA] as a truly, deeply evil organization. I agree with PETA that humans should treat animals better in a broad sense, but PETA's extremist and often criminal actions make them as alien to moderate vegetarians as they are to meat-eaters. Any group that opposes animal testing for life-saving medical purposes is deplorable.

My anti-PETA stance often gets me the instant, albeit fleeting, approval of meat-eaters. To them, I am one of the rare "reasonable ones," who are vegetarian perhaps by accident. This good impression lasts until I explain that, for most people, a vegetarian lifestyle is a morally superior choice. And while vegetarianism alone doesn't guarantee my moral fibre, it should count in my favour rather than against it.

Riva Gold, "COUNT HER FEET: The Moral High Ground Is Meatless," *McGill Tribune*, October 21, 2008. Reproduced by permission of the author.

The Moral Argument for Vegetarianism

We've all heard of vegetarianism's many moral perks. I won't explain all of them in detail, but consider two important ones: the meat industry is often incredibly cruel, and vegetarianism is much more environmentally sustainable. If you don't believe me, do some research. However, the main argument for vegetarianism's moral superiority is this: animals aren't necessarily equal to humans, but as sentient beings, we ought to care about them at least a little bit.

The main argument for vegetarianism's moral superiority is this: animals aren't necessarily equal to humans, but as sentient beings, we ought to care about them at least a little bit.

In his article, Eric wrote that "Eating meat is not wrong. Our ancestors ate meat in order to survive and we've inherited their place at the top of the food chain." Ah, the good old naturalistic fallacy. Being natural or traditional doesn't make something morally legitimate. This is especially true about eating meat, because the context of dietary decisions has changed dramatically in recent years. Our ancestors didn't have access to modern soy protein, vitamin supplements, and the like. Meat was often their only option. But just because meat was the right choice then doesn't mean it's the right choice now, when being vegetarian is easier than ever.

Don't get me wrong—like Eric, I think that humans are superior to animals. But our superiority isn't based on our place "at the top of the food chain." (Besides, any lion you meet alone in the jungle will beg to differ.) Humans are uniquely important because we're capable of making moral judgements. We have the capacity for compassion, for reason—in short, for humanity. Only humans can weigh the minor pleasure of eating beef against the pain and suffering that produced it.

Human superiority is precisely why we shouldn't be needlessly cruel to animals. We're not special because we happen to have a perch atop the food chain. We're special because only we are in a position to use our power ethically. For every cow we kill when we could easily eat tofu, for every chicken we needlessly coop up, we lose a little bit of our humanity.

Human superiority is precisely why we shouldn't be needlessly cruel to animals.

Aside from cases of anaemia and poverty, I have yet to hear a compelling moral argument for eating meat. And until I do, I will continue to take the moral, and distinctly human, high ground at every animal-free meal I enjoy.

Ultimately, every individual makes their own choices. I have no intention of joining radical, anti-meat protest groups, or proclaiming that animals are equal to humans. It's precisely because humans are not like other animals that we shouldn't be acting like them when we make dietary choices.

People Have a Moral Obligation to Reject Factory-Farmed Meat

Peter Singer

Peter Singer is a professor of bioethics at Princeton University, a well-known animal rights advocate, and a co-author of the book The Way We Eat: Why Our Food Choices Matter.

Global meat consumption is predicted to double by 2020. Yet in Europe and North America, there is growing concern about the ethics of the way meat and eggs are produced. The consumption of veal has fallen sharply since it became widely known that to produce "white"—actually pale pink—veal, newborn calves are separated from their mothers, deliberately made anemic, denied roughage, and kept in stalls so narrow that they cannot walk or turn around.

In Europe, mad cow disease shocked many people, not only because it shattered beef's image as a safe and healthy food, but also because they learned that the disease was caused by feeding cattle the brains and nerve tissue of sheep. People who naively believed that cows ate grass discovered that beef cattle in feed lots may be fed anything from corn to fish meat, chicken litter (complete with chicken droppings) and slaughterhouse waste.

Concern about how we treat farm animals is far from being limited to the small percentage of people who are vegetarians or even vegans. Despite strong ethical arguments for vegetarianism, it is not yet a mainstream position. More common is the view that we are justified in eating meat, as long as the animals have a decent life before they are killed.

The Problem of Industrial Meat Production

The problem, as Jim Mason and I describe in our recent book, *The Way We Eat*, is that industrial agriculture denies animals even a minimally decent life. Tens of billions of chickens produced today never go outdoors. They are bred to have voracious appetites and gain weight as fast as possible, then reared in sheds that can hold more than 20,000 birds. The level of ammonia in the air from their accumulated droppings stings the eye and hurts the lungs. Slaughtered at only 45 days old, their immature bones can hardly bear the weight of their bodies. Some collapse and, unable to reach food or water, soon die, their fate irrelevant to the economics of the enterprise as a whole.

The problem . . . is that industrial agriculture denies animals even a minimally decent life.

Conditions are, if anything, even worse for laying hens crammed into wire cages so small that even if there were just one per cage, it would be unable to stretch its wings. But there are usually at least four hens per cage, and often more. Under such crowded conditions, the more dominant, aggressive birds are likely to peck to death the weaker hens in the cage. To prevent this, producers sear off all birds' beaks with a hot blade. A hen's beak is full of nerve tissue—it is, after all, her principal means of relating to her environment—but no anesthetic or analgesic is used to relieve the pain.

Pigs may be the most intelligent and sensitive of the animals that we commonly eat. When foraging in a rural village, they can exercise that intelligence and explore their varied environment. Before they give birth, sows use straw or leaves and twigs to build a comfortable and safe nest in which to nurse their litter.

But in today's factory farms, pregnant sows are kept in crates so narrow that they cannot turn around, or even walk more than a step forward or backward. They lie on bare concrete without straw or any other form of bedding. The piglets are taken from the sow as soon as possible, so that she can be made pregnant again, but they never leave the shed until they are taken to slaughter.

As consumers, we have the power—and the moral obligation—to refuse to support farming methods that are cruel to animals and bad for us.

Defenders of these production methods argue that they are a regrettable but necessary response to a growing population's demand for food. On the contrary, when we confine animals in factory farms, we have to grow food for them. The animals burn up most of that food's energy just to breathe and keep their bodies warm, so we end up with a small fraction—usually no more than one-third and sometimes as little as one-tenth—of the food value that we feed them. By contrast, cows grazing on pasture eat food that we cannot digest, which means that they add to the amount of food available to us.

It is tragic that countries like China and India, as they become more prosperous, are copying Western methods and putting animals in huge industrial farms to supply more meat and eggs for their growing middle classes. If this continues, the result will be animal suffering on an even greater scale than now exists in the West, as well as more environmental damage and a rise in heart disease and cancers of the digestive system. It will also be grossly inefficient. As consumers, we have the power—and the moral obligation—to refuse to support farming methods that are cruel to animals and bad for us.

Vegetarianism Is the Right Moral Choice for Many Reasons

Brian Solomon

Brian Solomon lives in Madison, Wisconsin, and is a member of the Madison City Council.

Leo Tolstoy [a Russian author] said, "A vegetarian diet is the acid test of humanitarianism."

It is an interesting concept, that of connecting the food we eat to morality. When we look at it from an individualistic point of view, which is what we pretty much do, it's easy to just make the choice—to eat meat or not to eat meat. Because, like most other things, what difference does ONE person really make?

Like all other decisions, it's not that easy. When we look at what we eat from a broader perspective, and consider the realities involved in the decision, it provides a different picture.

- 9 billion chickens per year in factory farms will never have the chance to do one thing that is natural to them. They will never build a nest, take a dust bath, breathe fresh air, or meet their parents.

- 41 million cows will be burned and castrated, then transported to the slaughterhouse. Many die on the way. Those that don't are shot in the head with a bolt gun, hung by their legs, and then have their throats cut. They are often conscious through the entire process.

- 170,000 pigs die in transport each year, 420,000 are crippled by the time they reach the slaughterhouse. Many are still fully conscious when they are dipped in scalding water for hair removal.

Brian Solomon, "Ethics and Vegetarianism: Why What We Eat Matters," *Progressive Cogitation*, March 2006. Reproduced by permission.

- 300 million turkeys are killed each year in the US. Before this, their beaks and toes burned off with a hot blade, they are then crammed into filthy sheds.

- Every year in the laying industry, 280 million newly hatched male chicks—who can't produce eggs themselves—are thrown into garbage bags or grinders, to suffocate or be crushed or hacked to death.

This is an ethical conundrum right from the start, because we are incapable of meeting our own nutritional needs. We by default act against the interests of others in ensuring our survival. The dilemma is apparent from the get go—we must consume life to survive.

So is there a moral issue? How do we draw the line and decide that animals have some inherent right to life versus, say, a fruit or vegetable? There are several issues at hand.

The majority of us do not want animals to suffer, . . . [but we seem to be able to] detach from reality when the subject at hand has anything to do with our appetites.

Respect for Life

First, is respect for life. Humans proclaim to maintain a deep respect for life and I do believe, for the most part, this is true. But for some reason our stomachs seem to get in the way, and we use their likes and dislikes as our means for determining right and wrong. I say cannibalism and you say gross. Therefore we can clearly and quite easily place it in the "wrong" column. I say "dog meat" or "horse meat" and most of us have the same reaction. "Yuck" becomes equivalent to "wrong."

I say ribs, bacon cheeseburger, or tandoori chicken, and our reaction is completely different. Our moral opposition drains away in direct proportion to our salivation levels. And while I presume the majority of us do not want animals to suffer, it seems we have an internal on/off switch that allows us to detach from reality when the subject at hand has anything to do with our appetites.

Many cultures can maintain a deep respect for life and still take that very same life. An example is Native American cultures that only killed what they could eat, used every part of the animal, and said a blessing over every killing. Sadly, this would not be possible today without decreasing the amount of our consumption, vastly increasing the cost of meat, or harder yet, requiring a more personal connection to the animals we killed and ate.

We simply cannot truly respect and bless these animals, and by default their lives themselves, when the depth of our connection is a plastic wrapped, Styrofoam container full of hamburger, whose origin or journey we couldn't possibly fathom.

I know I could not kill an animal with my own hands—so why would I eat an animal just because someone else does it for me? [Animal rights activist and photographer] Linda McCartney once said, "if slaughterhouses had glass walls, everyone would be a vegetarian." What do you think she meant by this? My interpretation of this is that we simply would cease support our current treatment of animals if we had to participate more fully in the process.

The Moral Question

The second concept has to do with the moral question. Under what moral prerogative are we able to apply the tenets of equality, justice, and right to life to humans, and some animals (such as dogs, cats, and horses), but not the remainder of the animal kingdom?

Think about this quote by [philosopher and author] Peter Singer: "The animals themselves are incapable of demanding their own liberation, or of protesting against their condition with votes, demonstrations, or bombs. Human beings have the power to continue to oppress other species forever, or until we make this planet unsuitable for living beings. Will our tyranny continue, proving that we really are the selfish tyrants that the most cynical of poets and philosophers have always said we are? Or will we rise to the challenge and prove our capacity for genuine altruism by ending our ruthless exploitation of the species in our power, not because we are forced to do so by rebels or terrorists, but because we recognize that our position is morally indefensible?"

There is a principle called the "Sanctity of Life." [German theologian and doctor] Albert Schweitzer was a major proponent. His justification for the principle was the following: (a) I have a will to live, (b) When I am healthy and sincere towards myself, I feel reverence for my will to life, (c) All other organisms have a similar will to live, (d) I experience empathy with other life as I reflect honestly, dwelling on its similarity to my own life, (e) My empathy generates sympathy, caring, and a "compulsion" to approach other life with the same reverence I feel for my life, and (f) Hence, reverence for life is a fundamental virtue.

There is a commonly articulated criticism against vegetarians that they claim to respect life but nonetheless eat plants, and plants are living organisms too. There is some substance to this argument, but not much. The argument about right to life does not define life as merely "alive," but rather as sentience and consciousness. Few would argue that members of the plant kingdom have the same level of consciousness as animals. Additionally, many plants can easily weather the loss of an appendage, where as most animals cannot. And, of course, many plants make their usage as food beneficial not only to us, but to them as well. Bearing fruit is of course the most obvious and delicious example.

Some more moral food for thought:

- The first statement of Buddhism is "do not kill."

- Hindu scriptures recognize spirituality in all living things.

- The sixth commandment: "thou shalt not kill."

- Genesis: "To man and all creatures wherein is a living soul."

- The Bible also says that "man has dominion over the animals." But think of the meaning of the word "dominion." The Bible spends the majority of its words imparting a reverence for life. Kings and queens have dominion over their people, but I do not believe this imparts in them permission to torture, kill, eat, wear, or experiment on their subjects.

- An interesting quote by Reverend Andrew Linzey: "Animals are God's creatures, not human property, nor utilities, nor resources, nor commodities, but precious beings in God's sight. . . . Christians whose eyes are fixed on the awfulness of crucifixion are in a special position to understand the awfulness of innocent suffering. The Cross of Christ is God's absolute identification with the weak, the powerless, and the vulnerable, but most of all with unprotected, undefended, innocent suffering."

The Environmental Issue

The third issue deals with whether current behaviors are sustainable given their impact on the environment.

I know you've heard all these things before, but I think they bear repeating. As I read these, think about the staggering implications of each one . . . and the almost incomprehensible implications of them taken in sum.

- Of all agricultural land in the US, 80 percent is used to raise animals for food.

- It takes 2,500 gallons of water to produce a pound of meat, but only 25 gallons to produce a pound of wheat.

- Audubon estimates that 50% of the water used in the US is to raise animals for food.

- A vegetarian diet requires 300 gallons of water per day. A meat diet requires 4,000 gallons. That's a difference of 3,700 gallons a day or 26,000 gallons a week. For each person that would move to a vegetarian diet.

- 55 square feet of rain forest needs to be razed to produce a quarter pound hamburger.

- 360 million acres of forest in the US alone have been cleared for cropland for farmed animals. The Smithsonian says seven football fields of land on earth are bulldozed every minute to create room for farm animals.

- Farmed animals produce 130 times the excrement of the entire US human population—without sewage treatment. About 86,000 pounds per second. Much of it ends up in our water and soil. The EPA [U.S. Environmental Protection Agency] estimates that chicken, hog, and cattle excrement have polluted 35,000 miles of rivers in 22 states and contaminated groundwater in 17 states.

- 1/3 of the fossil fuels in the US go into the production of meat.

I know these numbers seem almost impossible to believe, but think about it this way. To eat a hamburger, these are the steps required:

- Grow tons of grain (tilling, irrigation, etc)

- Transport grain on 18 wheelers to feed mills

- Operate feed mills

- Transport feed to factory farms

- Operate factory farms

- Truck animals to slaughter

- Operate slaughterhouses

- Transport meat to processing plants

- Operate processing plants (There is an entirely additional, energy intensive process to create all the packaging needed)

- Transport meat to grocery stores

- Keep meat refrigerated or frozen until ready for use (Then there's the waste of all the packaging)

Meat animals of the world alone consume food equal to calorie needs of 9 billion people.

Here is a question: is it possible to be an environmentalist and a meat eater? In reality, there are few things we could do as a society that would have a more beneficial impact on the environment than to vastly decrease or eliminate our consumption of meat.

Effect on the Rest of the World

The fourth issue deals with whether current behaviors are sustainable given their impact on the remainder of humanity.

Animals raised for food are fed more than 70 percent of the grains the US produces. It takes 22 pounds of grain to produce one pound of meat.

Meat animals of the world alone consume food equal to calorie needs of 9 billion people.

There are estimates that the world currently produces enough vegetarian food to feed 15 billion people. 1.4 billion people could be fed with the grain and soybeans we feed US cattle alone. 40,000 children die of hunger every day.

We all know, of course, that distribution and politics are a big part of this problem, but are not solely responsible. Even if they were, and we can definitely discuss this topic, an ethical question remains: is it okay to engage in a behavior that wastes resources, when it is widely known that people are suffering and dying because of a lack of those very same resources?

[English singer/songwriter and peace/animal rights activist] Paul McCartney said: "If anyone wants to save the planet, all they have to do is just stop eating meat. That's the single most important thing you could do. It's staggering when you think about it. Vegetarianism takes care of so many things in one shot: ecology, famine, cruelty."

One could argue that eating meat, when one can meet their nutritional needs with a vegetarian diet, is akin to buying a Hummer when one really only needs a Corolla.

Waste and Over-Consumption

A fifth issue, related to the last couple, just deals with consumption.

I think it's mostly been covered already, especially in the environmental discussion. But I think it deserves it's own minute in the limelight. Most people would agree that consumption is, in many ways, related to both waste and equity. Over-consumption results inevitably in waste and, in a world of haves and have-nots, is clearly an equity issue.

Consumption is, thus, an ethical issue. I have a lot of thoughts on this, related to production, productivity, availability, and price, but I'll leave it with this: most of us believe we live in a nation that is heavy on consumption. In many ways, this is similar to our discussion. One could argue that eating meat, when one can meet their nutritional needs with a vegetarian diet, is akin to buying a Hummer when one really only needs a Corolla. Or to buying a mansion when one only needs a three bedroom.

I think we seldom think about it in those terms, but when one considers the 2500 gallons of water necessary to produce a pound of beef versus the 25 gallons needed to produce a pound of wheat, I don't think we can deny the depth of the similarity. . . .

We have clearly evolved to the point where a vegetarian diet is not only easy to come by, but better for the earth.

Time to Be Herbivores

In conclusion: There is a lot of talk about humans being omnivores. I think it likely that our omnivorous nature served us well during the evolution of our species. It seems likely that there were times in our evolution when our ability to derive nutritional value from as many sources as possible served as a critical survival mechanism.

However, it is clear that we have more in common with herbivores than carnivores, including our intestinal length, the strength of our stomach acid, the shape and size of our teeth and nails, the existence of sweat glands, and other features. And we have clearly evolved to the point where a vegetarian diet is not only easy to come by, but better for the earth, more sustainable for the environment and the long run survival of our species, and more justifiable on pretty much any moral basis.

If you do think we are truly carnivorous by nature, imagine a wolf or lion stumbling upon a day old cow carcass in the woods. Imagine the profound joy that this animal would feel upon its discovery. Now imagine how you'd react, were you to stumble across the same thing.

Now, with all that said, I not only think our omnivorous nature served us well in our evolution, but actually didn't contain the volume of moral issues that it does today. When there were fewer humans, each of whom was having a direct connection to the animals they killed and ate, one could certainly argue that the implications were not as dire.

Two examples of this still exist: consuming locally produced, free range, organic meat and hunting or fishing for your own food.

Organic farmers often, but not always, treat the animals with more respect and dignity, and actually offer them some quality of life. Most of the time, the environmental impacts are far less pronounced—though the reality remains: it will always take more land, water, and resources to produce an animal for food then it would to produce a vegetarian alternative. The other reality that remains is that we have to consciously make the moral decision that the life of an animal is not as meaningful as the life of a human.

Hunting and fishing are a different story. We might have other moral issues with these behaviors, but in many ways, they are the closest example of an equality-based paradigm. While we are still taking a life, and making the moral decision that that life is not as valuable as ours, we are at least offering full respect for the quality of that life prior to its taking. The animal has lived its life, and it's time has come. One could argue that, were it not a rifle or bow, it could have been a lion or wolf. No resources went into the production of this animal, and its life had full meaning until the very end.

I must allow that there is something to the concept that dying is okay when a life has been well-lived. It's not like we have a choice about the dying part. There is an ethical issue with leading a cow to a slaughterhouse, but I would argue, had that cow lived the good, true, and happy life of a cow, that the ethical issue is much diminished from the one we face with our current food production techniques.

With all that said, I think this issue comes down to three main questions:

- What is our moral responsibility to respect life, and how far does it extend?

- What is our ethical responsibility for our natural environment?

- And, what is price of our behavior on the human race?

I think we could all agree that there is an ethical responsibility on all of us to help those who cannot help themselves. Then the question asks how far down the food chain this must extend. Ethics is, in the end, almost always about choice. And with that, I leave you with an [philosopher] Albert Schweitzer quote: "A man is really ethical only when he obeys the constraint laid on him to aid all life which he is able to help."

Vegetarianism Is Part of Many Religious Traditions, Including Christianity

Kamran Pasha

Kamran Pasha is a Hollywood filmmaker and author.

I am not a vegetarian or a vegan. But like most people of conscience, I was sickened and horrified to see the recent [2009] video taken by animal rights activists of baby chicks being ground alive at an egg hatchery. Seeing such cruel and heartless treatment of living beings has undoubtedly caused some of us carnivores to at least take a moment to consider the dark truths behind how animals are processed for food in the modern world.

Indeed, human beings throughout history have questioned the morality of animal slaughter, and religious traditions such as Hinduism and Buddhism have long been the home for those who believe that killing and consuming sentient animals is barbaric. Religious vegetarianism is commonplace in the East, but is not considered mainstream in most Western faith communities.

And yet, after lengthy research into the historical record, I have become convinced that Jesus Christ himself was in all likelihood a vegetarian, and that vegetarianism was probably a central tenet of the early Christian community founded by his disciples. In fact, there is evidence that Christ's opposition to animal sacrifice at the Jewish Temple may have been the triggering event that led to the Crucifixion. . . .

Kamran Pasha, "Was Jesus a Vegetarian?" *The Huffingon Post*, September 3, 2009. Reproduced by permission of the author.

Jewish Christianity and Gentile Christianity: James Versus Paul

In order to get to the point that Jesus appears to have been a vegetarian according to early Christian sources, I must first give a basic explanation of the historical process by which the religious movement we now call Christianity came together. There are many sources for the following historical interpretation, but the most readable and well argued is by Prof. Barrie Wilson, a respected biblical scholar at York University in Toronto. His work *How Jesus Became Christian* provides a detailed examination of the evolution of Christian thought that I summarize below.

My investigation into the life of Jesus began by examining the first theological dispute that arose in the Christian community after the earthly mission of Jesus. Interestingly, there is little controversy over how Jesus lived. Most scholars, both secular and Christian, would likely accept the notion that Jesus in his lifetime was a practicing Jew, one who adhered to the Torah, the Law of Moses, even if he had some different interpretations of specific legal points than other Jewish teachers. That meant that Jesus was circumcised, prayed ritually every day according to ancient Jewish practices, worshipped at the Jewish Temple in Jerusalem, observed the Sabbath and major Jewish festivals such as Passover and Yom Kippur, and adhered to kosher laws regarding which foods were acceptable and which weren't.

This last point was not controversial in his lifetime, but became a major issue later when an increasing number of Gentiles (who had no such food restrictions) began to convert to Christianity. But during his lifetime, and for several years afterward, the followers of Jesus did not see themselves as creating a new religion. They were Jews who believed that Jesus was their teacher and leader, and the Acts of the Apostles discusses how the early Christians continued to worship at the Jewish Temple like other Jews, apparently unaware of the doctrine that Christ's death and resurrection removed the need to observe these ritual Jewish practices. This early "Jewish Christian" community was led by James the Just, identified in the New Testament as the younger brother of Jesus, and supported by well-known disciples like Peter and John.

According to contemporary historian Flavius Josephus, James the Just was highly respected by the Jewish community of Jerusalem for his righteousness and adherence to the Law of Moses. And yet modern Christians do not consider adherence to the Mosaic Law necessary or perhaps even virtuous. In fact most Christians today would be hard-pressed to name a handful of the 613 commandments that form the backbone of the Torah. So as I researched my novel [*Mother of the Believers*], the question naturally arose—how did Christianity transform from a community of Torah-observant Jews into a Gentile religion that renounced the Law of Moses?

The answer to that question comes in the figure of one man whose vision of the risen Christ changed the history of the world: the Apostle Paul. The story of Paul's conversion from a persecutor of Christianity to its greatest champion is famed in Church history and doctrine. On his way to arrest Christian fugitives in Damascus, Paul claimed to have a direct personal vision of Christ. The Acts of the Apostles and Paul's own letters differ in the exact details of this profound spiritual event, but the end result was clear. Paul said that he had been given a direct revelation of Christ's gospel and began to preach his understanding of Christ to Gentiles.

For Paul, Christ was more than a Jewish teacher and political leader, as the Jerusalem community around James believed. Christ was a Divine Being who had sacrificed his life to cleanse the world of sin. It is in Paul's letters that we first find the doctrines of Christ's divinity and vicarious atonement (the Gospels would be written later, when Paul's ideas had become prevalent among Christians). Paul taught his followers that obedience to the ritual law of Moses was no longer necessary—indeed it was a "curse". All that was needed to be a Christian was faith in Christ and his redemptive sacrifice.

These ideas have of course become the bedrock of modern Christianity. But what is fascinating is that Paul's letters, the earliest Christian documents (preceding even the Gospels by decades), reveal that Paul's vision of the Christ was not the same as the Jesus known to his family and disciples.

The Jesus Movement (Jews who saw Jesus as their teacher and leader) was based in Jerusalem at the time, while Paul was preaching to Gentiles throughout Asia Minor (modern Turkey), apparently without any authority from the disciples to do so. Indeed Paul proudly claims in his letters that he did not need anyone's authority to preach and that his Gospel came directly from Christ himself.

Not surprisingly, his proclamation of speaking on behalf of Christ did not sit well with the Jerusalem Christians who had known Jesus personally and could not reconcile Paul's vision of the antinomian [that faith alone is necessary for salvation] Christ with the Torah-observant rabbi who had led them. According to Paul's Letter to the Galatians, James the Just sent envoys to check up on him and what he was preaching. And when these envoys heard his doctrines, especially with regard to faith in Christ removing the need for Christians to follow Jewish dietary laws, all hell broke loose. As Paul himself describes the incident in Galatians, he had a shouting match with Peter and other disciples, and was very much the odd man out.

Several of Paul's letters in the New Testament were written to respond to the critiques of these Jewish Christians, who claimed Paul was misguided and perhaps even lying about his encounter with Christ. Indeed, the modern Christian notion that Paul was on good terms with the disciples who had known Jesus in his lifetime is simply not borne out in Paul's own letters. While the Acts of the Apostles, written years later by Paul's followers, often portrays the debates between James and Paul as cheerful disagreements between brothers, Paul's own letters show that their differences were intense and volatile. It was as if the two movements were actually competing religions rather than branches of the same faith.

How Pauline Christianity Triumphed

But if Paul's vision of Christ had little support from the people who actually knew Jesus, how did it become the basis for Christianity? The answer lies in the tragedy of the Roman destruction of Jerusalem in 70 C.E. The followers of Jesus the man were centered around Jerusalem, while the followers of Christ the God were scattered throughout the Roman Empire. The Jewish Christian community suffered a major blow when their leader James the Just was murdered in 62 C.E., and when the Roman legions destroyed Jerusalem and the Jewish Temple a few years later, the surviving Jewish Christians fled to Pella in modern Jordan.

The Ebionites were vegetarian, rejecting animal sacrifice as immoral, claiming again that they were following the teachings of Jesus himself.

The death of James and the destruction of Jerusalem crippled the Jesus Movement and placed it dangerously close to extinction. According to 4th century Christian historian Eusebius, the blood relatives of Jesus were hunted down as political threats by the Roman Emperors Domitian and Trajan and the people who had known and followed Jesus in his lifetime rapidly became an endangered species.

Paul's Christ Movement, on the other hand, was phenomenally successful. Untouched by the destruction of Jerusalem, the Gentile based religion easily eclipsed the struggling Jewish movement that had been its predecessor (and competitor). Paul's vision of Christ the Divine Savior had many similarities to popular religions of the Roman Empire, including the mystery schools of Egypt and the cult of Mithras. The ideas of a Divine Man incarnating, dying and being reborn, were already popular mystical doctrines in these communities, and it was not hard to replace Mithras or Osiris with Christ. And the end result was that over centuries, Paul's idiosyncratic view of Jesus became the orthodox Christian line, simply because it survived and thrived. . . .

The Ebionites and the Survival of Jewish Christianity

After the destruction of Jerusalem, the surviving Jewish Christians continued under a variety of names according to early Church historians. The most common name for these groups was the Ebionites, from the Hebrew word *Evyonim*, which means "the poor." This is an apparent reference to the many sayings of Jesus where he consistently honors and elevates the poor. . . .

Based on their Gospel, the Ebionites rejected what was becoming mainstream Christianity and denounced the letters of Paul as false teachings. The Ebionites faithfully observed the Law of Moses, claiming that in doing so, they were following the example not only of James, Peter and the disciples, but of Jesus himself. And according to Epiphanius, the Ebionites were vegetarian, rejecting animal sacrifice as immoral, claiming again that they were following the teachings of Jesus himself.

In the *Panarion*, his epic treatise against heresy, Epiphanius gives us many details about the Ebionite lifestyle. He says that the Ebionites claimed that the Apostle Peter had been a vegetarian and had ordered his followers to abstain from eating meat. In the Ebionite Gospel, they quote Jesus as saying "I came to abolish sacrifices, and unless you cease from sacrificing, my anger will not cease from you." The reference is to the practice of animal sacrifice in the Jewish Temple, where thousands of animals were ritually slaughtered every year as offerings to God, the meat being shared with the Priests.

Vegetarianism and compassionate treatment of animals was an important part of early Christian thought.

The Ebionites claimed that Jesus was horrified by cruelty to animals and that one of the primary aspects of his mission was to abolish the practice of ritual slaughter. Their argument was that Temple sacrifices were an innovation and had no basis in the authentic Law of Moses, and Jesus was sent to restore the Torah as Moses had practiced it. To the extent that the Jewish scriptures appeared to endorse animal sacrifice by the Priests, they claimed that such passages were forgeries inserted by the Priesthood itself to promote its livelihood. . . .

After having been confronted with this wealth of information about the Ebionites, who have a strong historical claim to be a continuation of the Jewish movement started by Jesus and subsequently led by James the Just, it became evident to me that vegetarianism and compassionate treatment of animals was an important part of early Christian thought. . . .

Was the Crucifixion the Result of Christ's Opposition to Animal Sacrifice?

The evidence that Jesus was a vegetarian, or at least early Christians who knew him were vegetarians, was compelling. But it seemed to be a minor doctrinal point, with little historical significance.

And then I came across a remarkable book called *The Lost Religion of Jesus: Simple Living and Nonviolence in Early Christianity* by Keith Akers, which posits a shocking thesis—that the central event of the Christian faith, the Crucifixion, was predicated upon Christ's willingness to fight for animal rights.

Akers is a committed vegetarian and he makes no apologies for the fact that he is evangelizing vegetarianism as a moral code for others. And some who read his book might find his persistence on the subject annoying. Regardless, the book truly makes compelling arguments that vegetarianism was intrinsic to Christ's message of love and compassion for the world, and that gentleness toward animals is a prominent theme in Christ's parables. Akers explains in greater depth the historical processes that I have detailed above, and the book is valuable for anyone who wishes to understand how the vision of Paul differed from that of other early Christians, and why Paul's vision ultimately triumphed to become Christian orthodoxy.

But for me, the most powerful argument that Akers makes is that Christ's rejection of animal sacrifice brought him into direct conflict with the Temple Priests, leading to Christ's arrest and trial under Pontius Pilate. Akers has the remarkable ability to point out evidence in the biblical texts that is hiding in plain site.

Most Christians would agree that the immediate event that led to Christ's arrest under the charge of sedition was his confrontation at the Temple. The famous scene where Jesus overturns the tables of the moneychangers is usually the focal point of Christian tellings of the story. Christ's attack on Temple business practices such as converting foreign exchange was seen as a threat to the Sadducee Priests' power, thus resulting in their willingness to turn him over to Pilate on the claim of fomenting rebellion against Rome.

And yet, as Akers points out, the moneychangers were a small part of the Temple scene. It is unlikely that the Priests would have felt directly threatened by an attack on unscrupulous traders overcharging pilgrims on exchange rates. But the Gospel accounts actually list moneychangers as one of several groups that Jesus drove out of the Temple—and they are not the first in line.

"Jesus entered the temple area and drove out all who were buying and selling there. He overturned the tables of the money changers and the benches of those selling doves." (Matthew 21:12)

The primary reference is to those who were "buying and selling." What does that mean? That means the huge business of animal sales for sacrifice! The Temple was both a site of worship and a butcher shop. Jesus was disrupting the Temple's primary revenue stream—the trade of animals for ritual slaughter.

That Jesus was primarily concerned with animal sacrifice in the Temple is made explicitly clear in the Gospel of John:

"When it was almost time for the Jewish Passover, Jesus went up to Jerusalem. In the Temple courts he found men selling cattle, sheep and doves, and others sitting at tables exchanging money. So he made a whip out of cords, and drove all from the temple area, both sheep and cattle; he scattered the coins of the moneychangers and overturned their tables. To those who sold doves he said, 'Get these out of here! How dare you turn my Father's house into a market!' His disciples remembered that it is written: 'Zeal for your house will consume me.'"

In the Gospel of John, Jesus physically drives herds of animals out of the Temple courtyard using a whip. It is an incredibly powerful visual image. Yet in all the years of that I have listened to the story of Jesus at the Temple, I have never heard anyone focus on this compelling scene. The overturning of the currency tables seems to be what is stuck in the Christian consciousness, and yet the most dramatic and chaotic event in this incident is clearly the freeing of the animal herds.

As Akers argues, the direct attack on the Priests principal source of livelihood, the animal sacrifices, could not be ignored. The Priests had to respond to the threat Jesus posed to their power, and they did. And the outcome changed the course of history.

What Does This Mean for Us Today?

If we accept that Jesus of Nazareth, the divine Savior of Christianity and the human Prophet of Islam, cared so deeply for animals that he would endanger his own life to end cruelty against them, what does that mean for us today?

Neither mainstream Christianity nor mainstream Islam endorses vegetarianism as a preferred lifestyle. But Akers makes a compelling argument that spiritual vegetarians have always existed within the Christian community, and that their voice of compassion toward animals is one that will never be silenced.

And Akers suggests convincingly that the Ebionites were ultimately absorbed into Islam, which shared most of their views about Jesus. And their vegetarian beliefs continued to influence Sufis, the mystics of Islam. Many Muslims would be surprised to learn that Rabia al-Adawiyya, a beloved female Sufi saint, was a vegetarian. And many Islamic legends around Jesus portray him as an ascetic who avoided meat and was deeply concerned for the welfare of animals as well as humans.

The barbaric practices of modern slaughterhouses violate the merciful traditions of Judaism, Islam, and yes, Christianity.

And so these teachings of Jesus continue to live on.

I think it is important to remember in a modern mechanized world, where animals are slaughtered in horrific ways using cruel and monstrous machines, that we do have a responsibility to other creatures on this earth. We have a duty to them, to our Creator, and to our own humanity, to show animals mercy and compassion. Watching beautiful little chicks ground alive by gears and blades should make us question who we are and what being human means.

On a personal note, I do not plan to renounce the consumption of meat. But I now have a preference to eat meat that has been slaughtered in as humane a way as possible. In both Judaism and Islam, there are ancient rules of sacrifice meant to lessen an animal's suffering and bring a quick and merciful death. Called *shechita* in Jewish kosher laws and *zabiha* in Islam's halal rules, these slaughter practices were developed in a primitive desert world where human survival should have been the only concern. And yet these ancient nomads chose to think about the welfare of animals, to feel empathy for the taking of their lives for food, and to find ways to do so as mercifully as they could. The barbaric practices of modern slaughterhouses violate the merciful traditions of Judaism, Islam, and yes, Christianity, and the holy figures of our traditions would undoubtedly reject such contemporary cruelties.

I would venture to guess that many Jews and Muslims living in the West today are lax about eating only meat that is kosher or halal. I know that is true in my own case. But after seeing some of the horrifying images from modern secular slaughterhouses, perhaps it is time for all of us to look into our religious histories and take seriously the traditions that emphasize mercy toward animals.

Maybe it is time to look back in order to move forward.

Killing Animals for Food Is Part of the Natural Order

Rebecca Thistlethwaite

Rebecca Thistlethwaite is a farmer, non-profit consultant, researcher, and mother.

My partner and I used to be vegetarians, coincidentally for the same exact amount of time—12 years. I began my vegetarianism as a college freshman working in the dining hall of my dormitory, horrified by the ingredients in the chicken nuggets and other 'meat-like' processed foods they offered there. It didn't help that I was putting on the dreaded 'freshman 15' so I thought cutting meat out of my diet would help for weight control (little did I know that my fake meat and carb-loading ways would actually fatten me up quicker!). I was getting into the whole hysteria over the destruction of the Amazon, which was being fueled by expanding cattle and soybean production around Brazil. At the time, it did not even enter my mind that there might be grassfed cattle operations within the same county as my university that were struggling to find buyers of their meat. I thought, meat was meat was meat and there were no choices, at least at the grocery stores I knew of.

I don't know what drew my partner to vegetarianism in the first place, but he too thought he would avoid meat to improve his health. However, with his limited cooking skills, he didn't exactly fill the meat void with steamed kale and lentil stew. He ate more starches, empty carbs, and found his energy lagging throughout the day. At the time he was even an ultramarathoner, fueling his body with weird energy elixers and gels to keep his body moving. He now thinks he would have

Rebecca Thistlethwaite, "The Meat We Eat: Part Three," *Honest Meat*, January 6, 2009. Reproduced by permission.

performed even better and won more races had he been gnoshing ham and cheese sandwiches or beef jerky for his 6–8 hour runs.

That animals kill other animals for food is a fact of nature.

The Natural Order of Things

When we started raising our own animals and killing our own animals, we felt like we could participate in eating them again. We have a reverence for our animals that people who pick up their identity-less 'meat' products at the grocery store or fast food restaurant will never know. So what about the morality of killing animals? Again, I turn to the next installment of *The River Cottage Meat Book* and Hugh Fearnley-Whittingstall's thoughtful words:

> "Such determined adherence to the vegetarian cause, at whatever cost, only brings us back to the irreducible, absolute moral position with which we started: that killing animals to eat them is always, and absolutely, wrong. Once the vegetarian position is reduced to this fundamentalist tenet, it becomes hard to counter rationally. But you can have an intuitive objection to such a moral absolute. Who says it's wrong? What makes it wrong? It doesn't strike me as in any way obvious that killing animals is, in itself, morally wrong. Particularly if we are killing them for food. We are not outside the natural order of things. And if we don't kill them for food, then somebody else, or something else, will.
>
> That may sound trite, but it is an important point in this discussion. That animals kill other animals for food is a fact of nature. That all animals will eventually die is another. A less obvious fact is that, of all the available deaths an animal can face in the wild, the most common, and probably the least traumatic, is death at the hands of another animal who

wants to eat it. 'Dying of old age' barely exists in nature. An animal suffering from injury or illness is likely to be killed by a predator before it finally succumbs to weakness or disease. And it will be eaten by something—the jackal, the vulture, or the maggot.

Humans and the animals they raise for food do not operate outside this natural sphere. We kill animals for food that would otherwise die another death. We are not taking life from the immortal. There are differences, though, between ourselves and the other potential killers of our livestock. One is that we tend to kill animals that are in the prime of life, whereas other predators favor the young, the weak, and the sick. But our preference for the healthy isn't a moral perversion: every predator would prefer a healthy animal to a diseased one, if it could catch it. And by killing animals before they begin to degenerate or get sick, we are arguably minimizing their pain and suffering, not increasing it.

Another difference is that we are, uniquely among meat eaters, not compelled to kill animals for food (although, as I have argued above, our ancestor probably had an irrefutable instinct to hunt prey). Another way of putting this is that we are the only predatory species with the capacity to refrain from doing what comes naturally. But does that mean that we should refrain? Not necessarily. After all, if the fate meted out by humans to the animals they kill for food is no worse, or perhaps demonstrably better, than that on offer from other potential killers, then isn't it morally preferable?

As it happens, the way in which we kill animals for food is quite different from that of other predators. We don't chase them down and tear them to death with our teeth and claws. We don't crush them to death, or swallow them alive. We corral them into groups, load them on to trucks, prod and poke them into a reasonably orderly queue, and then shoot them in the head with something called a captive bolt gun.

It is ironic, and also fairly astonishing, that the killing methods of many nonhuman predators are considered such a fascinating aspect of the natural world that films displaying them in graphic detail, often replaying the process several times in slow motion, are considred to be at the classy end of prime-time entertainment, fit for children as well as adults. Whereas the final moments of human predation of our farmed livestock are considered too disturbing and shameful to be made available even for information. In fact, such limited footage as does exist has often been filmed undercover and is more likely to be used to fuel the rage of the militant vegetarian than to educate us dispassionately about the way our meat is made.

There is no doubt that Western society is very confused about death—both human and animal death. Human death as dramatic entertainment in movies and on television has, like animal-on-animal predation, never been more familiar. Yet the human act of killing animals for food, once familiar to most of society, has now become so shameful that those who condone it—by eating meat every day—are entirely protected from thinking about it. Food animals are killed and their meat is cut up and packaged far from human eyes. By the time meat reaches the consumer, its animal origins have been all but obliterated."

Farm Animals Survive by Dying

Amy Standen

Amy Standen, along with Sasha Wizansky, founded the magazine Meatpaper *in 2006, and currently works as a reporter for* Quest, *KQED public radio's local science and environment program in northern California.*

It's one thing to rhapsodize about forging a connection to your food at the local farmers' market. It's another thing entirely to harvest that food from a rabbit hutch on the back porch.

Novella Carpenter is the only person I know who renders lard on her kitchen stove from pigs she raised out back. She's also the only person I know whose spring plans involve brain-tanning rabbit pelts that have dried stiff as boards in her over-stuffed refrigerator. But while straw piles up in the crooks of the stairway, and sacks of soon-to-be-cured olives hang from the pantry ceiling, the home Novella and her partner Bill share is far from rural: It's a one-bedroom apartment in a rough-and-tumble neighborhood of Oakland, California. Between the back porch, a small yard in the back, and an adjacent vacant lot where Novella grows vegetables, it's a complete, working farm in a very unlikely place.

On the winter solstice Novella slaughtered one of the turkeys she raised in her backyard and let *Meatpaper* photographer Julio Duffoo document the process. She and I met a few weeks after the slaughter, in a park in San Francisco's Mission District.

Amy Standen, "The Urban Farmer: Do Farm Animals Survive by Dying?" *Meatpaper*, March 2008. Reproduced by permission.

Amy Standen: *Tell us about this turkey.*

Novella Carpenter: I think there were six turkeys who came to us, and he was one of four who survived. They had a nice little flocking relationship. The garden was one of their favorite places to go. They'd march down the sidewalk, and they'd hang out and play in the garden until it was time to go back to their little area behind the house. When they were really little, one of the turkeys almost died. I came out one day and I found him flattened and freezing. I picked him up and brought him back to life, so maybe it was this one, I don't know.

Some animals are easier to kill than others. Birds are easier to kill than a mammal. With mammals, there's a closer connection to being human.

You can't tell them apart?

No, there were three bourbon reds, and they all look the same.

Did you name them?

The one we killed didn't have a name. A lot of farmers say you shouldn't name animals you're going to kill. Other people will say, "Boy, Oscar in the freezer is really delicious!" I have a friend who is adamant about naming the animal he's going to kill. He really pampers those animals and gives them the best possible life, because it's going to be a really short life. And I like that philosophy. But naming is for you; it's not for the animal. The animal doesn't [care] . . . if he has a name or not.

Is it hard for you to kill the animals?

It's not really hard, but, you know, every farmer says this: I don't look forward to it. Some animals are easier to kill than others. Birds are easier to kill than a mammal. With mammals, there's a closer connection to being human.

You were a vegetarian at some point, like a real "Meat is Murder" person.

I must have been about 16 when I started. I can't remember what it was I read, but my mom put a steak in front of me and I was like, "I just can't do it. This is an animal!" Then I was a vegetarian for about two years in college. So all told, maybe four years. Not that long.

And you were converted back by a plate of bacon in Las Vegas, right? What do you make of that vegetarian period now, looking back?

I think [my] philosophy was really juvenile. It's hoping something doesn't have to die. It's very "Babe" or "Charlotte's Web." But the final, logical conclusion to being a vegetarian or vegan is that farm animals will cease to exist.

Sure, but some people . . . have argued that a life lived for the purpose of dying is not a real life.

The final, logical conclusion to being a vegetarian or vegan is that farm animals will cease to exist.

I guess you could say that, but you're ignoring human culture. Animals and domesticated farm animals are tied together. They're interlocked; they've coevolved. We've made them exist, and they've helped us survive. And so for me, it's like, why don't we keep up that beautiful tradition? Part of that tradition is dying, but part of that is surviving. Those animals continue to exist because of us.

It's funny to see you positioned as this champion of carnivorism when you're such a conscientious meat eater—you pretty much only eat meat you kill yourself.

Pretty much. A lot of my vegan and vegetarian friends have told me, "This is the only acceptable way for you to eat meat." And I think that's true. You see the conditions that [factory-farmed animals live] in. If it's this mindless thing where you don't know where the meat came from, you don't know how it died or anything about it, to me that's kind of gross.

But there's a reason most people don't know anything about how their food animals die—it's an upsetting thing to see. And you're someone who has always felt a strong connection to animals.

That's part of the reason I sort of build a ritual around [the slaughter], burn tobacco, etc. Obviously, the ritual is for us, not the animal, but there needs to be a boundary between regular life and killing something. That's one reason that factory farming is so horrible: The animals are part of a machine, and you're just a cog in that machine, you're part of it, too. The turkey doesn't care if we thank him, obviously. But the ritual is to keep human, it's to admit to ourselves what we're doing is something that needs to be forgiven. It's also reminding yourself this isn't a normal part of your life.

But at the same time, I know you feel that slaughter is a very normal part of life.

We've made [farm animals] exist, and they've helped us survive.

It's the logical conclusion of six months of life, or so, for an animal. The problem that people have is that they aren't there every day. They don't see the turkey every day. Every single day I saw this turkey. I fed him; I cleaned up after him; I picked him up and held him; I gave him water. You watch them grow and then it's time. They aren't children. They aren't babies that you're going to, like, educate or whatever. They're farm animals, and that's what they're here for. This is what they do. And so you're harvesting them like an apple or anything else you've been cultivating. That's what humans do, and that's how we are able to eat.

They aren't pets. It's always been like this from the very beginning; for every animal we had I was always really clear that this was its purpose. That's why this animal was here. They reach a plateau where they aren't going to get any bigger, they're not going to taste good anymore, and it's just like wasting food if you keep feeding them. So there's a moment when you just have to say: I've got to do this.

It's true that generations and generations of that animal have, unless they're breeders, only lived to a certain age. So in a way, that is the end of the lifecycle. But it's hard to call it a "natural" life-cycle.

Right. Well, animals in the wild die really early. I think humans are still trying to figure out if we're part of nature or not.

You're harvesting [farm animals] like an apple or anything else you've been cultivating. . . . That's how we are able to eat.

Your parents were back-to-the-landers in Idaho. Do you see what you're doing now as part of that tradition, transplanted to West Oakland?

The problem with the back-to-the land blueprint is that it requires you to live in the country with a bunch of hillbillies you don't want to live with. And basically, it was total isolation for my parents, even though their ideals—to grow their own food—were laudable. To me, urban farming is that perfect combination of doing what my parents wanted to do: having a relationship with my food, while simultaneously staying in the city, keeping a job, and having interactions with people from different cultures. It's the good things about the city and the good things about the country together.

The Internet has changed it. You can order poultry online. I'm buying goats from a woman I found on Craigslist. The Internet is the modern Whole Earth Catalogue, except it allows you to customize urban farming. The *Whole Earth Catalog* was like a blueprint; it would say: "You will raise rabbits." People are more free-thinking now.

When I visit you I'm always struck by how much work it is to run a farm out of one's apartment.

I guess so, but it's not work, like, "go to your job." You can do it whenever you want. So I'll go pick stuff for the rabbits at midnight, for example. Some animals, like the pigs, are a huge amount of work, but then you never have to go to the grocery store. For me, hell is the grocery store. You drive to the store, stand in line, wander around in that soul-sucking place, and buy a bunch of crap you don't need just because you happen to be there.

Last July I spent a month living entirely off the garden, and I felt like I had tons of free time. If I wanted food I just walked downstairs and ate a bunch of food.

That sounds wonderful, but I can't imagine people doing what you do on a mass scale.

In Third World counties, urban farming is huge, but they don't call it "urban farming." They just live with the goats in the house because it's practical. So many people are moving from the country to the city, the density staggering, but they're keeping their culture, too. So they're going to raise goats even if those goats live on the roof, or there are ducks in the bath-tub.

It's not part of our culture, although I would argue that, more and more, it's going to be part of our culture. That's the future. It's not going to be "Blade Runner" where everything's dead. It's going to be crammed with animals. Because there's not enough farmland for everyone to live like this.

And not enough oil to transport the food from the farms to the cities.

Yep. It's all going to be super localized, I think. People will [see pictures of cities] and be like, "What? There used to not be goats in these alleys?" What a waste of space! I look out at this park we're sitting in, and I can imagine a couple sheep out here.

It Is Moral to Eat Humanely Raised Meat

Douglas Brown

Douglas Brown is a lifestyle reporter and blogger for The Denver Post *newspaper.*

We all have heard horror stories about the way livestock are sometimes raised in this country: chickens stuffed into cages for their short lives, pigs never allowed to see the sky or feel the sun on their backs, thousands of cattle standing shoulder-to-shoulder in pens knee-deep in mud and their own waste.

I don't know much about these places, called concentrated animal feeding operations. Are the stories true? I have not done enough homework and am not qualified to pass judgment.

I am familiar, on the other hand, with a single ranch on an Indian reservation in Wyoming where the cattle spend most of their lives roaming a sprawling range of grass, where osprey and eagles wheel above cows and calves and wolves and bears. I am comfortable with Arapaho Ranch, a place that nurtures its cattle until the day they are shipped off to slaughter.

Working on the cover story for this week's Food section changed the way I buy food.

I eat meat. I savor how it tastes, I appreciate its textures, I sometimes feel compelled toward it, especially if I encounter the aromas from somebody's backyard barbecue.

But I feel compassion toward the animals I consume too.

After spending time on Arapaho Ranch, I believe I can reconcile my carnivorous ways with that which comes before I take my first bite: the animal's slaughter.

Humanely Raised Meat

What meat do I eat now? Meat from animals that were raised humanely. I guess that makes me a "humane-itarian."

This demands research on my part. It asks more of my wallet, which means I'll eat less meat. It turns restaurant-dining, for the most part, into an adventure in vegetarianism. It could make for uncomfortable dinner parties ("Was this chicken raised humanely? You don't know? Oh, OK. I'll just have the carrots."). Fortunately, my wife, Annie, is a vegetarian and all of our friends know it. So I'll just have what she's having. Unless, that is, the host announces he is serving meat from animals that were raised humanely.

[Eating only humanely raised meat] asks more of my wallet, which means I'll eat less meat.

The approach does raise an obvious question: If you respect the animals so much, why do you endorse their slaughter? What is humane about killing a living creature? It is a conundrum for which I do not have an easy answer.

But I'll give it a shot.

I believe carnivore is in my bones. I do not wish to reject my nature, but I am willing to put limits on it (I do this already in other realms: I sometimes feel driven toward, for example, cold beer; in middle-age I have grown to understand this drive needs limits).

It is important, I believe, to respect meat, to shrink from anything that cheapens the deaths of animals for our benefit.

So I will eat meat. And at the same time I will try, at least, to support farming and ranching that treat animals with deep respect and compassion.

CHAPTER 3

Is Vegetarianism More Environmentally Sustainable Than a Meat Diet?

Chapter Preface

Most of the beef that consumers buy in U.S. supermarkets is produced by more than half a million U.S. cattle farms and ranches. These ranches breed cows to produce calves, which typically graze with their mothers in herds on large grass pastures until they are weaned. After weaning, at about ten months old, the calves are sold to other ranchers and producers who begin preparing the cattle for their transfer to a feedlot, which occurs when the calves are between twelve and eighteen months of age. At the feedlot, the cattle are kept in pens and fed grains for several more months to fatten them, at which point they are sent to meat packing plants for slaughter. This system of beef production is the legacy of a colorful tradition of cowboys and cattle ranching in the American West that dates back to the mid-1800s.

Cattle were first brought to North America at the end of the fifteenth century by European explorers. By the early 1800s, numerous cattle ranches existed in northern Mexico, where a sturdy type of cattle called longhorns were raised on the open range and were guarded by cowboys called vaqueros. When Texas became a U.S. state in 1845, this style of open ranching continued, but during the U.S. Civil War (1861–1865) many ranches suffered as men volunteered to be soldiers and the economy in the southern states declined. As a result, cattle on open ranges were often left to fend for themselves—a neglect that, ironically, helped the herds to multiply rapidly. According to some estimates, by 1865 there were about 5 million longhorn cattle roaming free in Texas. Since there was great demand for beef in the Northeast, livestock traders looked for a way to connect the cattle in Texas with eastern markets. They offered large rewards to cowboys who could bring herds of longhorn cattle to places like Abilene, a small frontier town in Kansas located on the Kansas-Pacific railway.

From about 1867 until the early 1880s, millions of longhorn cattle were driven by cowboys from Texas to Abilene and other Midwestern cow towns, and then shipped east by train. On the trip north, the cattle fed on natural grasses that covered public lands in the Plains states. The development of refrigerated railroad cars in 1878 allowed the cattle to be slaughtered before shipping, creating large meatpacking industries in both Kansas and Chicago.

The era of the open range was short-lived, however. More people settled and began farming on the Plains; the invention of barbed wire allowed more areas to be fenced; a major drought struck the Midwest; and long cattle drives slowly became more difficult and less profitable. Eventually, ranchers began to breed heftier, less wild types of cattle and fenced them into defined ranges where they could be fed, watered, and protected. Cattle ranching became a popular business throughout the western Plains states, with ranches owned by families or partners.

The spread of cattle ranching, however, soon caused overgrazing, because cattle were often grazed year-round and the native grasses were never given a chance to renew themselves. Farming and sheepherding practices also killed the prairie grasses, as did a series of droughts. The final day of reckoning came in the 1930s with the Dust Bowl, a series of huge dust storms that swept across Midwest. With the grasses gone, there was nothing to hold the soil in place, and over a period of about six years, the winds blew dust as far east as Washington, D.C. The dust storms forced hundreds of thousands of people from their homes and left vast areas of land barren and uninhabited. The federal government's response was the Bankhead-Jones Farm Tenant Act of 1937, under which it reacquired some of the range and farm lands that had been abandoned and began an effort to restore native grasslands. In addition, Congress passed the Taylor Grazing Act of 1934, a law that gave government agencies the authority to manage public lands, grant grazing rights to ranchers, and impose grazing fees.

The Taylor Grazing Act and later legislation created today's system of allowing privately owned cattle to graze on public lands in a regulated fashion and for a fee. According to the Natural Resources Defense Council, cattle grazing is the main economic use of U.S. public lands, taking up approximately 260 million acres. Over the years, the grazing fees have been increased. Western ranchers object to what they consider high fees as well as to the fact that the federal government owns over one-half of the land in the western states. Ranchers see themselves as good stewards of the land and the government as a threat to the western way of life and the cowboy heritage. Ranches, they say, are the best way to stave off housing developments and urban sprawl, which pose the biggest danger to the environment and endangered species. Ranchers also argue that, by controlling vegetation growth, grazing helps prevent fires, and that it creates high-quality protein foods from low-quality grasses. Ranchers believe they know best how to manage the grasslands environment, and would like to have greater, not less, control over their grazing lands.

The view of most environmentalists, however, is that cattle grazing continues to harm the environment in the West. According to ranching critics, cattle are a non-native species that have a larger impact on the environment than native species. For example, unlike elk and deer, which move around so that they do not overgraze or cause soil damage, cattle typically stay in the same grazing area until they have eaten all available vegetation. This overgrazing, in turn, causes soil erosion and drought. In addition, environmentalists say that cattle compact the soil, trample vegetation and waterfowl nesting sites, deposit large amounts of polluting manure and urine in pristine natural areas, destroy streams and wetlands, and compete with wildlife for food, water, and space. According to environmental reports, many species of native plants and animals are already disappearing from western ranges, and hundreds of millions of acres of public lands are turning into deserts. Environmentalists also say that federal lands are leased at far less than their fair market value and that grazing fees are so low that they amount to a massive subsidy to the cattle industry. They point out that the receipts from grazing fees do not even begin to cover the basic costs of managing and improving federally owned ranges. Many environmentalists would like to see the West preserved for wildlife and intact ecosystems.

Whether livestock helps or harms the environment is one of the important issues being raised by vegetarians. The authors of the viewpoints in this chapter debate whether vegetarianism is more environmentally sustainable than a meat diet.

The Livestock Sector Is a Major Source of Environmental Degradation

Henning Steinfeld, Pierre Gerber, Tom Wassenaar, Vincent Castel, Mauricio Rosales, and Cees de Haan

Henning Steinfeld, Pierre Gerber, Tom Wassenaar, Vincent Castel, Mauricio Rosales, and Cees de Haan work in the livestock sector analysis and policy branch at the Food and Agriculture Organization of the United Nations in Rome, Italy.

The livestock sector emerges as one of the top two or three most significant contributors to the most serious environmental problems, at every scale from local to global. The findings of this report suggest that it should be a major policy focus when dealing with problems of land degradation, climate change and air pollution, water shortage and water pollution and loss of biodiversity.

Livestock's contribution to environmental problems is on a massive scale and its potential contribution to their solution is equally large. The impact is so significant that it needs to be addressed with urgency. Major reductions in impact could be achieved at reasonable cost.

Global Importance of the Sector

Although economically not a major global player, the livestock sector is socially and politically very significant. It accounts for 40 percent of agricultural gross domestic product (GDP) [a measure of a country's total economic output]. It employs 1.3 billion people and creates livelihoods for one billion of the world's poor. Livestock products provide one-third of

Henning Steinfeld, Pierre Gerber, Tom Wassenaar, Vincent Castel, Mauricio Rosales, and Cees de Haan, *Livestock's Long Shadow: Environmental Issues and Options*, Rome, Italy: Food and Agriculture Organization of the United Nations, 2006. Reproduced by permission.

humanity's protein intake, and are a contributing cause of obesity and a potential remedy for undernourishment.

The environmental impact per unit of livestock production must be cut by half, just to avoid increasing the level of damage beyond its present level.

Growing populations and incomes, along with changing food preferences, are rapidly increasing demand for livestock products, while globalization is boosting trade in livestock inputs and products. Global production of meat is projected to more than double from 229 million tonnes [a unit of mass equal to 2204.6 pounds] in 1999/01 to 465 million tonnes in 2050, and that of milk to grow from 580 to 1043 million tonnes. The environmental impact per unit of livestock production must be cut by half, just to avoid increasing the level of damage beyond its present level.

Structural Changes and Their Impact

The livestock sector is undergoing a complex process of technical and geographical change, which is shifting the balance of environmental problems caused by the sector.

Extensive grazing still occupies and degrades vast areas of land; though there is an increasing trend towards intensification and industrialization. Livestock production is shifting geographically, first from rural areas to urban and peri-urban, to get closer to consumers, then towards the sources of feedstuff, whether these are feedcrop areas, or transport and trade hubs where feed is imported. There is also a shift of species, with production of monogastric species (pigs and poultry, mostly produced in industrial units) growing rapidly, while the growth of ruminant production (cattle, sheep and goats, often raised extensively) slows. Through these shifts, the livestock sector enters into more and direct competition for scarce land, water and other natural resources.

These changes are pushing towards improved efficiency, thus reducing the land area required for livestock production. At the same time, they are marginalizing smallholders and pastoralists, increasing inputs and wastes and increasing and concentrating the pollution created. Widely dispersed non-point sources of pollution are ceding importance to point sources that create more local damage but are more easily regulated.

Livestock production accounts for 70 percent of all agricultural land and 30 percent of the land surface of the planet.

Land Degradation

The livestock sector is by far the single largest anthropogenic user of land. The total area occupied by grazing is equivalent to 26 percent of the ice-free terrestrial surface of the planet. In addition, the total area dedicated to feedcrop production amounts to 33 percent of total arable land. In all, livestock production accounts for 70 percent of all agricultural land and 30 percent of the land surface of the planet.

Expansion of livestock production is a key factor in deforestation, especially in Latin America where the greatest amount of deforestation is occurring—70 percent of previous forested land in the Amazon is occupied by pastures, and feedcrops cover a large part of the remainder. About 20 percent of the world's pastures and rangelands, with 73 percent of rangelands in dry areas, have been degraded to some extent, mostly through overgrazing, compaction and erosion created by livestock action. The dry lands in particular are affected by these trends, as livestock are often the only source of livelihoods for the people living in these areas.

Overgrazing can be reduced by grazing fees and by removing obstacles to mobility on common property pastures. Land degradation can be limited and reversed through soil conservation methods, silvopastoralism, better management of grazing systems, limits to uncontrolled burning by pastoralists and controlled exclusion from sensitive areas.

The livestock sector is a major player [in climate change], responsible for 18 percent of greenhouse gas emissions.

Atmosphere and Climate

With rising temperatures, rising sea levels, melting icecaps and glaciers, shifting ocean currents and weather patterns, climate change is the most serious challenge facing the human race.

The livestock sector is a major player, responsible for 18 percent of greenhouse gas emissions measured in CO_2 [carbon dioxide] equivalent. This is a higher share than transport.

The livestock sector accounts for 9 percent of anthropogenic CO_{2r} emissions. The largest share of this derives from land-use changes—especially deforestation—caused by expansion of pastures and arable land for feedcrops. Livestock are responsible for much larger shares of some gases with far higher potential to warm the atmosphere. The sector emits 37 percent of anthropogenic methane (with 23 times the global warming potential (GWP) of CO_2) most of that from enteric fermentation by ruminants. It emits 65 percent of anthropogenic nitrous oxide (with 296 times the GWP of CO_2), the great majority from manure. Livestock are also responsible for almost two-thirds (64 percent) of anthropogenic ammonia emissions, which contribute significantly to acid rain and acidification of ecosystems.

This high level of emissions opens up large opportunities for climate change mitigation through livestock actions. Intensification—in terms of increased productivity both in livestock production and in feedcrop agriculture—can reduce greenhouse gas emissions from deforestation and pasture degradation. In addition, restoring historical losses of soil carbon through conservation tillage, cover crops, agroforestry and other measures could sequester up to 1.3 tonnes of carbon per hectacre per year, with additional amounts available through restoration of desertified pastures. Methane emissions can be reduced through improved diets to reduce enteric fermentation, improved manure management and biogas—which also provide renewable energy. Nitrogen emissions can be reduced through improved diets and manure management.

The Kyoto Protocol's [an international treaty on climate change] clean development mechanism (CDM) can be used to finance the spread of biogas and silvopastoral initiatives involving afforestation and reforestation. Methodologies should be developed so that the CDM can finance other livestock-related options such as soil carbon sequestration through rehabilitation of degraded pastures.

The livestock sector is a key player in increasing water use, . . . mostly for the irrigation of feedcrops.

Water

The world is moving towards increasing problems of freshwater shortage, scarcity and depletion, with 64 percent of the world's population expected to live in water-stressed basins by 2025.

The livestock sector is a key player in increasing water use, accounting for over 8 percent of global human water use, mostly for the irrigation of feedcrops. It is probably the largest sectoral source of water pollution, contributing to eutrophication, "dead" zones in coastal areas, degradation of coral reefs, human health problems, emergence of antibiotic resistance and many others. The major sources of pollution are from animal wastes, antibiotics and hormones, chemicals from tanneries, fertilizers and pesticides used for feedcrops, and sediments from eroded pastures. Global figures are not available but in the United States, with the world's fourth largest land area, livestock are responsible for an estimated 55 percent of erosion and sediment, 37 percent of pesticide use, 50 percent of antibiotic use, and a third of the loads of nitrogen and phosphorus into freshwater resources.

Livestock also affect the replenishment of freshwater by compacting soil, reducing infiltration, degrading the banks of watercourses, drying up floodplains and lowering water tables. Livestock's contribution to deforestation also increases runoff and reduces dry season flows.

Water use can be reduced through improving the efficiency of irrigation systems. Livestock's impact on erosion, sedimentation and water regulation can be addressed by measures against land degradation. Pollution can be tackled through better management of animal waste in industrial production units, better diets to improve nutrient absorption, improved manure management (including biogas) and better use of processed manure on croplands. Industrial livestock production should be decentralized to accessible croplands where wastes can be recycled without overloading soils and freshwater.

Policy measures that would help in reducing water use and pollution include full cost pricing of water (to cover supply costs, as well, as economic and environmental, externalities), regulatory frameworks for limiting inputs and scale, specifying required equipment and discharge levels, zoning regulations and taxes to discourage large-scale concentrations close to cities, as well as the development of secure water rights and water markets, and participatory management of watersheds.

Biodiversity

We are in an era of unprecedented threats to biodiversity. The loss of species is estimated to be running 50 to 500 times higher than background rates found in the fossil record. Fifteen out of 24 important ecosystem services are assessed to be in decline.

Livestock now account for about 20 percent of the total terrestrial animal biomass, and the 30 percent of the earth's land surface that they now pre-empt was once habitat for wildlife. Indeed, the livestock sector may well be the leading player in the reduction of biodiversity, since it is the major driver of deforestation, as well as one of the leading drivers of land degradation, pollution, climate change, overfishing, sedimentation of coastal areas and facilitation of invasions by alien species. In addition, resource conflicts with pastoralists threaten species of wild predators and also protected areas close to pastures. Meanwhile in developed regions, especially Europe, pastures had become a location of diverse long-established types of ecosystem, many of which are now threatened by pasture abandonment.

Some 306 of the 825 terrestrial ecoregions identified by the Worldwide Fund for Nature (WWF) [an environmental group]—ranged across all biomes and all biogeographical realms, reported livestock as one of the current threats. Conservation International has identified 35 global hotspots for biodiversity, characterized by exceptional levels of plant endemism and serious levels of habitat loss. Of these, 23 are reported to be affected by livestock production. An analysis of the authoritative World Conservation Union (IUCN) Red List of Threatened Species shows that most of the world's threatened species are suffering habitat loss where livestock are a factor.

Since many of livestock's threats to biodiversity arise from their impact on the main resource sectors (climate, air and water pollution, land degradation and deforestation), major options for mitigation are detailed in those sections. There is also scope for improving pastoralists' interactions with wildlife and parks and raising wildlife species in livestock enterprises.

Reduction of the wildlife area pre-empted by livestock can be achieved by intensification. Protection of wild areas, buffer zones, conservation easements, tax credits and penalties can increase the amount of land where biodiversity conservation is prioritized. Efforts should extend more widely to integrate livestock production and producers into landscape management.

Cross-Cutting Policy Frameworks

Certain general policy approaches cut across all the above fields. A general conclusion is that improving the resource use efficiency of livestock production can reduce environmental impacts.

While regulating about scale, inputs, wastes and so on can help, a crucial element in achieving greater efficiency is the correct pricing of natural resources such as land, water and use of waste sinks. Most frequently natural resources are free or underpriced, which leads to overexploitation and pollution. Often perverse subsidies directly encourage livestock producers to engage in environmentally damaging activities.

A top priority is to achieve prices and fees that reflect the full economic and environmental costs, including all externalities. One requirement for prices to influence behaviour is that there should be secure and if possible tradable rights to water, land, use of common land and waste sinks.

Damaging subsidies should be removed, and economic and environmental externalities should be built into prices by selective taxing of and/or fees for resource use, inputs and wastes. In some cases direct incentives may be needed.

Payment for environmental services is an important framework, especially in relation to extensive grazing systems: herders, producers and landowners can be paid for specific environmental services such as regulation of water flows, soil conservation, conservation of natural landscape and wildlife habitats, or carbon sequestration. Provision of environmental services may emerge as a major purpose of extensive grass-land-based production systems.

An important general lesson is that the livestock sector has such deep and wide-ranging environmental impacts that it should rank as one of the leading focuses for environmental policy: efforts here can produce large and multiple payoffs. Indeed, as societies develop, it is likely that environmental considerations, along with human health issues, will become the dominant policy considerations for the sector.

Finally, there is an urgent need to develop suitable institutional and policy frameworks, at local, national and international levels, for the suggested changes to occur. This will require strong political commitment, and increased knowledge and awareness of the environmental risks of continuing "business as usual" and the environmental benefits of actions in the livestock sector.

A Vegetarian Diet Is More Energy Efficient Than a Meat Diet

University of Chicago News Office

The University of Chicago News Office serves as a media relations and editorial resource for University of Chicago faculty and administrators, as well as a clearinghouse of news and other information concerning the research activities of the university.

The food that people eat is just as important as what kind of cars they drive when it comes to creating the greenhouse-gas emissions that many scientists have linked to global warming, according to a report accepted for publication in the April [2006] issue of the journal *Earth Interactions*.

Vegan Diets Better for Environment

Both the burning of fossil fuels during food production and non-carbon dioxide emissions associated with livestock and animal waste contribute to the problem, the University of Chicago's Gidon Eshel and Pamela Martin wrote in the report.

The average American diet requires the production of an extra ton and a half of carbon dioxide-equivalent, in the form of actual carbon dioxide as well as methane and other greenhouse gases compared to a strictly vegetarian diet, according to Eshel and Martin. And with Earth Day approaching on April 22, cutting down on just a few eggs or hamburgers each week is an easy way to reduce greenhouse-gas emissions, they said.

"We neither make a value judgment nor do we make a categorical statement," said Eshel, an Assistant Professor in Geophysical Sciences. "We say that however close you can be

University of Chicago News Office, "Study: Vegan Diets Healthier for Planet, People Than Meat Diets," April 13, 2006. Reproduced by permission.

to a vegan diet and further from the mean American diet, the better you are for the planet. It doesn't have to be all the way to the extreme end of vegan. If you simply cut down from two burgers a week to one, you've already made a substantial difference."

The average American drives 8,322 miles by car annually, emitting 1.9 to 4.7 tons of carbon dioxide, depending on the vehicle model and fuel efficiency. Meanwhile, Americans also consume an average of 3,774 calories of food each day.

In 2002, energy used for food production accounted for 17 percent of all fossil fuel use in the United States. And the burning of these fossil fuels emitted three-quarters of a ton of carbon dioxide per person.

That alone amounts to approximately one-third the average greenhouse-gas emissions of personal transportation. But livestock production and associated animal waste also emit greenhouse gases not associated with fossil-fuel combustion, primarily methane and nitrous oxide.

"An example would be manure lagoons that are associated with large-scale pork production," Eshel said. "Those emit a lot of nitrous oxide into the atmosphere."

While methane and nitrous oxide are relatively rare compared with carbon dioxide, they are—molecule for molecule— far more powerful greenhouse gases than carbon dioxide. A single pound of methane, for example, has the same greenhouse effect as approximately 50 pounds of carbon dioxide.

The vegetarian diet turned out to be the most energy-efficient, followed by poultry and the average American diet.

Comparing Diets

In their study, Eshel and Martin compared the energy consumption and greenhouse-gas emissions that underlie five diets: average American, red meat, fish, poultry and vegetarian (including eggs and dairy), all equaling 3,774 calories per day.

The vegetarian diet turned out to be the most energy-efficient, followed by poultry and the average American diet. Fish and red meat virtually tied as the least efficient.

The impact of producing fish came as the study's biggest surprise to Martin, an Assistant Professor in Geophysical Sciences. "Fish can be from one extreme to the other," Martin said. Sardines and anchovies flourish near coastal areas and can be harvested with minimal energy expenditure. But swordfish and other large predatory species required energy-intensive long-distance voyages.

Martin and Eshel's research indicated that plant-based diets are healthier for people as well as for the planet.

"The adverse effects of dietary animal fat intake on cardiovascular diseases is by now well established. Similar effects are also seen when meat, rather than fat, intake is considered," Martin and Eshel wrote. "To our knowledge, there is currently no credible evidence that plant-based diets actually undermine health; the balance of available evidence suggests that plant-based diets are at the very least just as safe as mixed ones, and most likely safer."

In their next phase of research, Eshel and Martin will examine the energy expenditures associated with small organic farms, to see if they offer a healthier planetary alternative to large agribusiness companies. Such farms typically provide the vegetables sufficient to support 200 to 300 families on plots of five to 10 acres.

"We're starting to investigate whether you can downscale food production and be efficient that way," Martin said.

Vegetarianism Is One of the Most Effective Ways to Fight Global Warming

Ben Adler

Ben Adler is an urban leaders fellow at Next American City, *a national magazine that focuses on urban policy in the United States.*

These days almost any proposal to reduce global warming gets taken seriously, even by conservatives. Solar panels are proposed for powering everything except submarines. Oilman T. Boone Pickens wants to put windmills on every empty patch of land in Texas, and Republicans have finally found something to like about France: nuclear power.

But when Rajendra Pachauri, who runs the Intergovernmental Panel on Climate Change (IPCC), made a suggestion that could reduce global greenhouse gas emissions by as much as 18 percent, he was excoriated. Why was his proposal so unpalatable? Because he suggested eating less meat would be the easiest way people could reduce their carbon footprint, with one meat-free day per week as a first step. "How convenient for him: He's a *vegetarian*," sneered a *Pittsburgh Tribune Review* editorial. "Dr. Pachauri should be more concerned about his own diet. A new study shows that a deficiency of vitamin B-12, found primarily in meat, fish and milk, can lead to brain shrinkage." Boris Johnson, London's outspoken mayor, posted a long screed on his blog, declaring, "The whole proposition is so irritating that I am almost minded to eat more meat in response."

Ben Adler, "Are Cows Worse Than Cars?" *American Prospect*, vol. 19, December 3, 2008.

Johnson may not appreciate the environmental value of replacing his steak and kidney pie with a tofu scramble, but the benefits would be quite real. Animal agriculture is responsible for local pollution from animal waste and chemical use and for greenhouse gas emissions from the energy-intensive process of growing feed and raising livestock, plus the, ahem, byproducts of animal digestion. It would be much easier—and cheaper—to give up meat than to, say, convert an entire country's electrical grid to using solar, wind, or nuclear energy. A rural Montanan might have no choice but to drive to work, but he can certainly switch out his pork chop for pinto beans. While Pachauri was correct to note that one need not go vegan to help the environment—simply eating *less* meat would help—he could have also emphasized the more politically appealing point that one can be a carnivore and still reduce one's impact by choosing different meats. Even limiting one's meat consumption to chicken yields major environmental benefits—not to mention health and financial benefits.

Animal agriculture is responsible for local pollution from animal waste and chemical use and for greenhouse gas emissions.

What should be a surprise is not that Pachauri made the comments he did but that it took him so long to do so. In fact, the environmental movement has largely ignored meat consumption. The man with whom the IPCC shared its Nobel Prize for raising climate change awareness, Al Gore, has never mentioned the environmental impact of meat consumption. Green groups tell their conscientious constituents to trade in their SUV [sport utility vehicle] for a Prius [Toyota's hybrid electric car] and buy compact-fluorescent light bulbs but haven't dared suggest that they give up steak.

Perhaps even more so than cars, meat is deeply embedded in American culture. Apple pie may be the quintessential

American food, but McDonald's hamburgers aren't far behind. We carve turkey on Thanksgiving and host Fourth of July barbeques. Without meat, how do you know it's a meal? To most Americans, veggies and tofu are a laughable substitute. "It was a reaction to the '60s hippie cooking that gave this important idea of vegetarianism a bad name," says Alice Waters, the chef and author who is widely credited with creating the organic-food revolution. Environmentalists, who know they must change the stereotype that they are all either tree-hugging radicals or self-righteous scolds, may be reluctant to embrace vegetarianism because of those easily caricatured cultural connotations.

The environmental movement has largely ignored meat consumption.

"Environmental groups don't want to come out too strongly on it," says Danielle Nierenberg, who researches the intersection of animal agriculture and climate change for both the Humane Society, an organization that promotes the compassionate treatment of animals, and the World Watch Institute, an environmental think tank. "People get very upset when they feel they are being told what to eat."

Now should be environmental vegetarianism's big moment. Global warming is the single biggest threat to the health of the planet, and meat consumption plays a bigger role in greenhouse gas emissions than even many environmentalists realize. The production and transportation of meat and dairy, particularly if you include the grains that are fed to livestock, is much more energy-intensive than it is for plants. Animals, especially cattle, also release gases like methane and nitrous oxide that, pound for pound, are up to 30 times more damaging than carbon dioxide. Internationally there is an additional cost to animal agriculture: massive deforestation to make land available for grazing, which releases greenhouse gases as the trees are burned and removes valuable foliage that absorbs carbon dioxide. As a result, according to a 2006 United Nations [UN] report, internationally the livestock sector accounts for 18 percent of all greenhouse gas emissions—more than the transportation sector.

The numbers for the United States are more hotly contested. The Environmental Protection Agency (EPA) has estimated that meat is only half of the U.S. agriculture sector's share of domestic greenhouse gases and that the entire agriculture industry produces 7.56 percent of the U.S.' contribution. This is considerably less than the transportation sector, which the EPA estimates accounts for roughly 29 percent of U.S. greenhouse gas emissions. The American Meat Institute, an industry trade association, cites the EPA numbers as credible. But they fail to take into account that 50 percent of grain is being fed to livestock and that its production and transportation costs should also be attributed to what you find in the meat or dairy aisle of the supermarket. Additionally, the EPA numbers do not include large categories such as the transportation of plants and animals.

If all Americans ate a vegan diet it would cut greenhouse gas emissions by at least 6 percent, probably more.

In fact, some environmentalists allege that the [President George W.] Bush administration's EPA chose the lowest possible estimate, which the meat industry routinely cites, for political reasons. "With the EPA being in the pocket of the meat industry, it's not in their interest to come up with the best numbers," says Bruce Friedrich, who works on environmental issues for People for the Ethical Treatment of Animals.

The real U.S. figure is roughly halfway between the UN's and the EPA's numbers, according to independent experts. "There are many assumptions that one needs to make when quantifying emissions," explains Gidon Eshel, an environmental studies professor at Bard College at Simon's Rock. "It's not that any one assumption is correct. Almost all of them are defensible." Eshel estimates that if you used the UN's standards, animal agriculture would account for 10 percent or 11 percent of U.S. greenhouse gases.

Consumers may not have a say in whether or not another coal power plant will be built, but they do have control over how much meat they personally eat. A University of Chicago study co-authored by Eshel found that, for the average American, "the greenhouse gas emissions of various diets vary by as much as the difference between owning an average sedan versus a Sport Utility Vehicle." One meat eater going vegetarian results in putting the equivalent of 1.5 fewer tons of carbon dioxide into the atmosphere annually. Further, according to the study, if all Americans ate a vegan diet it would cut greenhouse gas emissions by at least 6 percent, probably more. Those savings would have a more immediate impact than would reducing the same amount of carbon through other means, because the average time scale for removing carbon dioxide from the atmosphere is about 10 times as slow as for methane. Most important, as Eshel notes, one can reduce personal greenhouse gas emissions through dietary change more easily and comfortably than, say, cutting back on electricity use by living in the dark or forgoing air conditioning all summer.

But meat eating has grown dramatically in developed countries in recent decades, with developing countries beginning to catch up. The average American eats 200 pounds of meat, poultry, and fish per capita per year, 50 pounds more than Americans did in the 1950s. Between 1970 and 2002 the average person in a developing country went from consuming 24 pounds to 65 pounds of meat annually. In all, the world's total meat consumption in 2007 was estimated to be 284 million tons, compared to 71 million tons in 1961. It is expected to double by 2050. "You're seeing now India and China, with a growing middle class, are eating more meat," says Laura Shapiro, a culinary historian and author of *Something from the Oven*, about the cuisine of 1950s America.

Yet the environmental conversation remains solely about cars and power plants, not beef and pork.

Unlike the vitriol that Rajendra Pachauri encountered, Caryn Hartglass has been met with a different reaction when she suggests people eat less meat: deafening silence. Hartglass is the only paid staffer for Earth Save, the most prominent organization dedicated solely to promoting an animal-free diet for environmental reasons. "I go to [environmental organizations'] Web sites and it's supposed to tell you what to do to reduce global warming and it doesn't say eat less meat," says Hartglass. "So I ask them why not. They say they're focusing on reducing carbon-dioxide emissions not methane-gas emissions."

Why are environmental groups and even politicians willing to tell Americans to drive smaller cars or take the bus to work but unwilling to tell them to eat less meat? If you live in a recently built suburb you must drive most places whether you wish to or not. Walking or public transit simply isn't an option. But you could stop buying ground beef and start buying veggie burgers tomorrow, saving yourself some money and sparing yourself some cholesterol in the process. And yet no one, other than a small cadre of lonely fringe activists like Hartglass, devotes much energy to making the connection. Food experts and environmentalists generally worry that Americans might react with hostility similar to Boris Johnson's if asked to put down their hamburgers.

Their timidity is understandable. On the rare occasion that the federal government has tried to even suggest that Americans lower their meat consumption, it has failed. In 1977, the Senate Select Committee on Nutrition and Human Needs recommended eating less meat and dairy to combat heart disease. But the meat and dairy lobbies complained vociferously, and the committee rephrased the report to say that people should instead choose animal products that would "reduce saturated fat consumption." Just to be sure no one else got the foolish idea of suggesting Americans eat less meat, the beef industry spent heavily to successfully defeat Committee Chairman George McGovern in 1980.

But while politicians may have reason to fear the meat lobby, environmental groups are supposed to push the political envelope. They began calling for caps on carbon emissions in the late 1990s, before it was politically palatable, and both major party candidates for president endorsed cap-and-trade in 2008. Many people see their car or truck as a part of their identity, but that hasn't stopped the Sierra Club from ensuring that every American is aware of the environmental threat their vehicle poses. And yet, the major environmental groups have been unwilling to push the meat issue. "I don't know of anyone in the environmental community that has taken a stance of 'we support no meat consumption because of global warming,'" says Tim Greef, deputy legislative director for the League of Conservation Voters. Adds Nierenberg, "It's the elephant in the room for environmentalists. They haven't found a good way to address it."

The Sierra Club's list of 29 programs—which includes such relatively small-bore issues as trash-transfer stations (they threaten "quality of life and property values")—does not include any on the impact of meat consumption. Their main list of things you can do to help prevent global warming mentions hanging your clothes out to dry instead of using a dryer but makes no mention of eating less meat. "The Sierra Club isn't opposed to eating meat, so that's sort of the long and short of it. [We are] not opposed to hunting, not opposed to ranching," says Josh Dorner, a spokesman for the Sierra Club, the nation's oldest and largest grass-roots environmental organization.

Of course, asking Americans to eat less meat is not the same thing as actively condemning ranching and hunting, but ranchers and hunters might consider it a threat to their livelihood and lifestyle all the same. And there's the rub. Though the Sierra Club does not have a position on meat consumption, it does ally with small ranchers and hunters on an array of issues, from opposing the development of giant feedlots to preserving land. "We believe that making connections with hunters and anglers is critical to ultimately getting a solution to global warming," says Dave Hamilton, director of the global warming and energy program at the Sierra Club. "They are often in places that are targets for what we're trying to do, and they are a key constituency for policy makers."

Calling for less meat consumption would almost certainly endanger that relationship. But the Sierra Club denies that is the reason for its lack of a stance on meat, saying that it focuses instead on issues where it can have a greater impact. "It does not necessarily pay to appear to be telling people how to live their lives," says Hamilton. "We want to give positive solutions. We've tried to focus on the things that we feel can make the greatest difference with the energy and resources that we have."

Other environmental groups, such as Natural Resources Defense Council [NRDC], acknowledge that reducing meat consumption would be helpful in ameliorating emissions, but it simply is not a high priority. "We haven't taken a position [on meat]," says Elizabeth Martin Perera, a climate-policy specialist at the NRDC. "There's no reason not to; we just haven't gotten around to it." The League of Conservation Voters, which coordinates environmental political efforts, explains it as a process of fighting one battle at a time. "Once you deal with the largest emitters of carbon, complementary policies need to get passed," says Greef. "After they pass cap-and-trade, you will see work for a better transportation bill, work on deforestation and the logging industry. Meat falls into that bucket."

When it comes to sorting out legislative priorities, Greef's position is sensible. The car-dependence of the American landscape and other energy-intensive consumption habits make attacking those larger emitters a higher priority domestically.

But environmental groups do more than just lobby Congress. First and foremost, they explain how our activities affect the environment. It is obvious that a car spews pollution, but to see your beef burrito first as a burping cow, and before that as oil being burned to grow corn to feed that cow, requires education. The movement also can advise the public on lifestyle choices and demonstrate how those choices can be practical. A typical Sierra Club member cannot do much to pass cap-and-trade, but she can skip the bacon in her breakfast sandwich.

Remember those TV commercials that declared, "Beef, it's what's for dinner"? Only a few foods are so central to American cuisine and culture that they can assert their primacy simply by reminding you that you've always consumed them. Americans do indeed eat an extraordinary amount of meat, roughly twice their daily recommended dose of protein. But contrary to the commercial, this was not always the case—consumption has not just been driven by market demand. The other culprit is cheap corn.

Meat has become cheaper—and therefore more prevalent in American diets—in the last 30 years because it has been heavily subsidized, albeit indirectly. Ever since Secretary of Agriculture Earl Butz declared in 1973 that "what we want out of agriculture is plenty of food," American agricultural policy has encouraged overproduction and lower prices, primarily in the form of massive subsidies for corn. Livestock, in turn, consumes more than half the corn grown in the U.S. because it is cheaper to confine animals to a tight lot and funnel corn in than to allow them to graze freely on grass. With cheaper grain and denser, dirtier feedlots replacing free-range ranches, meat prices and meat quality have dropped, while meat's environmental impact has increased.

"The livestock doesn't get direct subsidies per se, but they have until recently done very well by getting subsidized corn," says Larry Mitchell, director of government affairs at the American Corn Growers Association (ACGA), a rival offshoot of the National Corn Growers Association (NCGA), which the ACGA contends represents agribusiness conglomerates rather than small farmers. "Most of the huge, confined animal-feeding operations, factory farms, wouldn't be viable if they had to pay the true cost of corn," Mitchell says.

Some environmental scientists contend that, in addition to filling local groundwater with animal waste and destroying the open spaces of the West with feedlots, grain-fed meat creates more emissions per pound than grass-fed meat. "Some work from the EPA suggests that you can reduce methane by half by not confining animals and not feeding them high-energy grains," says Nierenberg. But, she concedes, the evidence is mixed. Other studies, such as those promoted by conservatives, find the opposite: Eating grass gives cows gas. A spokesperson for the NCGA declined to comment for this article but referred me to Alex Avery, a researcher at the conservative Hudson Institute. Avery, who acknowledges that his research is underwritten by industry interests, cites studies suggesting that corn-fed livestock emits less methane.

Our over-consumption of factory-farmed animals is the product of a set of indirect subsidies that make its cost artificially low.

Fundamentally, though, Avery and food-industry spokespeople don't acknowledge the role that cheap corn plays in the prevalence of meat in the American diet. "The world needs to eat," says Tamara McCann Thies, chief environmental counsel for the National Cattlemen's Beef Association, "and demand dictates how much beef is produced in the U.S. and elsewhere." Of course, demand is a product of price, and price is a product of production costs, and production costs are affected by subsidies. The world needs to eat, but it does not need to eat burgers.

Indeed, while a public-relations campaign would have some marginal impact, it has long been established that only government regulation can be certain to change America's consumption patterns. Despite all the publicity surrounding the ills of oil, average auto fuel efficiency has stagnated. And how many people do you know who hang-dry their clothes to keep the polar ice cap afloat?

So what would a political agenda to reduce the emissions from animal agriculture look like? The answer is surprisingly simple.

As with so many environmentally damaging habits, such as driving, our over-consumption of factory-farmed animals is the product of a set of indirect subsidies that make its cost artificially low. Much of the agriculture industry is exempt from compliance with the Clean Air and Clean Water Acts, thus reducing its business costs. Grain subsidies lower the cost of feed. And the Government Accountability Office recently found that the EPA has failed to hold factory farms accountable for massive violations, essentially another form of government subsidy by freeing them of the cost of compliance. Undoing any of these boondoggles would raise the cost of meat. Another option is to raise the standards of animal treatment, which would also make the production of meat more expensive. California recently passed a ballot proposal to ban cruelly overcrowded conditions in factory farms. By eliminating dense feedlots, which animal-rights activists and even many farmers regard as inhumane and which create local pollution, it should become more expensive to produce meat because it will require more land per animal. Although it is not clear how much meat consumption would fall as a result, it makes sense, as it does with driving, to at least remove the price advantage of such an environmentally destructive activity.

And, of course, the government could remove corn subsidies. Whatever the merits of grass-fed versus grain-fed meat, an increase in the price of corn would mean more expensive meat. But the institutional barriers to removing subsidies— the key committee positions of senators from farm states, the power of the Iowa caucuses, the political largesse of agriprocessor Archer Daniels Midland—make such a dramatic reversal in American agricultural policy an incredibly tall order. In any case, the environmental movement has not shown any desire to make this a top priority.

In the meantime, activists are taking small bites out of the problem. Food experts like Shapiro and Waters say that raising awareness about reducing portion size, which has grown over the years, is one first step. And a Web site called PB&J Campaign, launched in February 2007, encourages a plant-based diet for environmental reasons. Bernard Brown, the site's 31-year-old creator, says he is careful to advocate not outright vegetarianism but intermediate steps that are more realistic.

Yet they still have a long way to go. "I think it's amazing that even the greenest of green liberal environment activists, the vast majority of them tend to consume meat at the same rate as people who think global warming is a hoax," says Mike Tidwell, director of the Chesapeake Climate Action Network. "Meat consumption seems to be the last thing that progressive people address in their lifestyle. If I had a nickel for every global warming conference that had roast beef on the menu, I'd be rich."

Vegetarianism Is Needed to Reform Industrial Meat Production

James E. McWilliams

James E. McWilliams is an associate professor of history at Texas State University at San Marcos, a fellow in the agrarian studies program at Yale University, and the author of the book Just Food.

I gave a talk in South Texas recently on the environmental virtues of a vegetarian diet. As you might imagine, the reception was chilly. In fact, the only applause came during the Q&A period when a member of the audience said that my lecture made him want to go out and eat even more meat. "Plus," he added, "what I eat is my business—it's personal."

Diets Are Political

I've been writing about food and agriculture for more than a decade. Until that evening, however, I'd never actively thought about this most basic culinary question: Is eating personal?

We know more than we've ever known about the innards of the global food system. We understand that food can both nourish and kill. We know that its production can both destroy and enhance our environment. We know that farming touches every aspect of our lives—the air we breathe, the water we drink, and the soil we need.

So it's hard to avoid concluding that eating cannot be personal. What I eat influences you. What you eat influences me. Our diets are deeply, intimately and necessarily political.

James E. McWilliams, "Bellying Up to Environmentalism," *The Washington Post*, November 16, 2009. Reproduced by permission of the author.

Evils of the Meat Industry

This realization changes everything for those who avoid meat. As a vegetarian I've always felt the perverse need to apologize for my dietary choice. It inconveniences people. It smacks of self-righteousness. It makes us pariahs at dinner parties. But the more I learn about the negative impact of meat production, the more I feel that it's the consumers of meat who should be making apologies.

Here's why: The livestock industry as a result of its reliance on corn and soy-based feed accounts for over half the synthetic fertilizer used in the United States, contributing more than any other sector to marine dead zones. It consumes 70 percent of the water in the American West—water so heavily subsidized that if irrigation supports were removed, ground beef would cost $35 a pound. Livestock accounts for at least 21 percent of greenhouse-gas emissions globally— more than all forms of transportation combined. Domestic animals—most of them healthy—consume about 70 percent of all the antibiotics produced. Undigested antibiotics leach from manure into freshwater systems and impair the sex organs of fish.

Our diets are deeply, intimately and necessarily political.

It takes a gallon of gasoline to produce a pound of conventional beef. If all the grain fed to animals went to people, you could feed China and India. That's just a start.

Meat that's raised according to "alternative" standards (about 1 percent of meat in the United States) might be a better choice but not nearly as much so as its privileged consumers would have us believe. "Free-range chickens" theoretically have access to the outdoors. But many "free-range" chickens never see the light of day because they cannot make it through the crowded shed to the aperture leading to a patch of cement.

"Grass-fed" beef produces four times the methane—a greenhouse gas 21 times as powerful as carbon dioxide—of grain-fed cows, and many grass-fed cows are raised on heavily fertilized and irrigated grass. Pastured pigs are still typically mutilated, fed commercial feed and prevented from rooting—their most basic instinct besides sex.

Vegetarianism is not only the most powerful political response we can make to industrialized food. It's a necessary prerequisite to reforming it.

Animal Suffering

Issues of animal welfare are equally implicated in all forms of meat production. Domestic animals suffer immensely, feel pain and may even be cognizant of the fate that awaits them. In an egg factory, male chicks (economically worthless) are summarily run through a grinder. Pigs are castrated without anesthesia, crated, tail-docked and nose-ringed. Milk cows are repeatedly impregnated through artificial insemination, confined to milking stalls and milked to yield 15 times the amount of milk they would produce under normal conditions. When calves are removed from their mothers at birth, the mothers mourn their loss with heart-rending moans.

Then comes the slaughterhouse, an operation that's left with millions of pounds of carcasses—deadstock—that are incinerated or dumped in landfills. (Rendering plants have taken a nose dive since mad cow disease.)

Now, if someone told you that a particular corporation was trashing the air, water and soil; causing more global warming than the transportation industry; consuming massive amounts of fossil fuel; unleashing the cruelest sort of suffering on innocent and sentient beings; failing to recycle its waste; and clogging our arteries in the process, how would you react? Would you say, "Hey, that's personal?" Probably not. It's more likely that you'd frame the matter as a dire political issue in need of a dire political response.

Vegetarianism Is the Answer

Vegetarianism is not only the most powerful political response we can make to industrialized food. It's a necessary prerequisite to reforming it. To quit eating meat is to dismantle the global food apparatus at its foundation.

Agribusiness has been vilified of late by muckraking journalists, activist filmmakers and sustainable-food advocates. We know that *something* has to be done to save our food from corporate interests. But I wonder—are we ready to do what must be done? Sure, we've been inundated with ideas: eat local, vote with your fork, buy organic, support fair trade, etc. But these proposals all lack something that every successful environmental movement has always placed at its core: genuine sacrifice.

Until we make that leap, until we create a culinary culture in which the meat-eaters must do the apologizing, the current proposals will be nothing more than gestures that turn the fork into an empty symbol rather than a real tool for environmental change.

\

Meat Can Be Part of a Sustainable Food System

Bill Niman and Nicolette Hahn Niman

Nicolette Hahn Niman lives in Bolinas, California, with her husband, Bill Niman, founder of Niman Ranch, a natural meat company supplied by a network of over six hundred traditional farmers and ranchers. Together, the Nimans have launched a new natural meat company called BN Ranch. Nicolette Hahn Niman is also an environmental lawyer, writer, and author of the book Righteous Porkchop: Finding a Life and Good Food Beyond Factory Farms.

Chefs and farmers gathered recently [2009] in Chicago to exchange ideas about making the food system healthier and more environmentally sustainable. The summit was hosted by Chefs Collaborative, a Boston-based non-profit. Panels and workshops ranged from butchering whole hogs to food production's role in global warming.

Meat Can Be Good for the Environment

Nicollete led a discussion focused on meat. Because there seems to be a growing perception that meat is inherently bad for the environment, she posed the question: Can meat be part of a sustainable food system? She led off with her own answer, an emphatic "YES!" It all depends on how and where animals are raised, and how meat is used. "Environmentally beneficial farming mimics natural ecosystems," she said. "Healthy ecosystems involve plants and animals functioning together."

Moreover, environmental statistics about meat production are often misunderstood. Take global warming. Because the

Bill Niman and Nicolette Hahn Niman, "Is Meat Bad for the Environment?" *The Atlantic Monthly*, October 1, 2009. Reproduced by permission of the authors.

greatest portion of meat's global warming contribution comes from deforestation in Latin America, India, and Asia, domestically-produced meat is unconnected to those emissions. Additionally, livestock raised without being fed fertilized crops are unrelated to another large part of the global warming equation: fossil fuel-based agricultural chemicals.

Nicolette also suggested that some animals are more easily raised in an environmentally benign way. Goats, for instance, can be raised entirely on naturally-occurring vegetation. Even better, goats prefer to eat woody brush that other grazing animals don't like. Thus, a cattle ranch can raise goats and cattle on the same pastures, making more efficient use of the land and naturally occurring vegetation.

Sustainable cooking means using meat that was raised using traditional methods and cutting back on portion sizes.

She also urged that sustainable cooking means using meat that was raised using traditional methods and cutting back on portion sizes. "Eat less meat. Eat better meat," she encouraged.

Tony Maws, chef and owner of the Cambridge, MA restaurant Craigie on Main, and Matt McMillin, inventor of the big bowl concept, added the chef's perspective to the discussion. Tony talked about cooking with the whole animal, which makes it possible to purchase directly from smaller farms and puts every part of the animal—from nose to tail—to good use. Tony said that he and his sous chefs spend much of their time honing their butchering skills.

As a consultant to restaurants and former partner in the restaurant group Lettuce Entertain You, Matt has spent much of his career helping restaurants make their menus, especially their meat, more environmentally friendly. Greening menus will not succeed without a commitment to "telling the story," Matt said. "Educating the front of the house is absolutely essentially," he emphasized.

The panel was rounded out by Will Harris, a fourth-generation cattle farmer from Georgia. Will Harris described his own transformation from commodity beef producer into grass-fed organic farmer. Meat from his farm costs more now, he explained, because he no longer relies on the short-cuts of hormones and antibiotic feeding.

The meat session's lively dialogue was typical of the Chefs Collaborative conference, which was infused with a palpable enthusiasm. It was heartening to know that chefs are returning to their communities energized with new ideas and inspiration for sustainability. The Chefs Collaborative board has decided to make the summit an annual event.

Meat Production Has Nothing to Do with Global Warming

Alan Caruba

Alan Caruba is the founder of The National Anxiety Center, a Web site dedicated to debunking claims made by environmental and consumer organizations.

In August 2007, Claudia H. Deutsch of *The New York Times* wrote an article titled "Trying to Connect the Dinner Plate to Climate Change." Talk about grasping at straws!

This alleged science writer was apparently unaware the Earth has been cooling since 1998 and a legion of scientists, climatologists, and meteorologists has blasted great big holes in the global warming hoax.

"The biggest animal rights groups do not always overlap in their missions," wrote Deutsch, "but now they have coalesced around a message that eating meat is worse for the environment than driving. They and smaller groups have started advertising campaigns that try to equate vegetarianism with curbing greenhouse gases."

Anti-Meat Party Line

Deutsch quoted Matt A. Prescott, manager of vegan campaigns for People for the Ethical Treatment of Animals (PETA), as saying, "You just cannot be a meat-eating environmentalist."

She also cited a Web page quoting Paul Shapiro, senior director of the Humane Society's campaign against factory farming, as asserting, "switching to a plant-based diet does more to curb global warming than switching from an S.U.V. to a Camry."

Alan Caruba, "Meat-Based Diets Benefit the Environment," *Environment & Climate News*, March 2009. Reproduced by permission.

Such claims are so absurd they challenge credulity—even if we ignore the fact that carbon dioxide (CO_2) increases have no effect on the warming of the Earth, as CO_2 constitutes only a tiny 0.038 percent of the Earth's atmosphere. The absurd claims are, however, part and parcel of the general attacks on the production and consumption of beef.

Those who raise livestock for America's dinner plates are ... more rightfully [qualified] to be called environmentalists than those seeking to convince people their diet is contributing to a bogus global warming crisis.

Nutritional Abundance

Americans have grown accustomed to the "food police," groups forever warning about eating just about anything and who complain Americans are suffering "an obesity epidemic." Michael Jacobson of the Center for Science in the Public Interest, for example, has opined that Americans should eat like eighteenth century serfs, dining "on perhaps a pound of bread, a spud, and a couple of carrots a day."

Such a diet could be imposed only by sheer force. According to the U.S. Department of Agriculture's Economic Research Service (ERS), U.S. consumers spend a smaller percentage of their disposable income on food consumed at home (6.5 percent) than any other nation in the world.

The abundance of a wide variety of nutritious and delicious beef and other meat items in supermarkets across the United States is a triumph of science and animal husbandry. Some 800,000 producers of beef not only feed Americans but also help the economy through their exports.

Stewards of the Land

Those who raise livestock for America's dinner plates are also strong stewards of the land and more rightfully qualify to be called environmentalists than those seeking to convince people their diet is contributing to a bogus global warming crisis.

More than half the agricultural land in America is unsuitable for raising crops. Grazing cattle is an example of responsible land management and has been practiced for hundreds of years. Grazing allows the land to remain productive while battling erosion, invasive plant species, and wildfires, thus protecting water and encouraging the growth of natural grasses.

Health Benefits

Despite these important environmental benefits, beef producers and farmers remain the targets of animal rights activists and environmental groups who consciously ignore the fact that food is required for human life while focusing all their attention on the energy required to produce it.

Yet the health benefits of beef products cannot be denied. They provide the nutrients for energy with a lower intake of calories than plants do, and they contribute a range of vitamins and minerals for a healthy lifestyle.

Beef production has nothing to do with global warming because there is no significant human-induced global warming.

This doesn't stop the propagandists from claiming meat is responsible for a variety of cancers and other alleged health threats.

The vegans will not tell you that diets rich in meat are a major factor in the regeneration of blood and in tissue repair. As a tissue builder of muscles and other elements, meat has no equal. Meat is easily digestible because the human body is designed to process it. The human body literally requires less effort to convert meat than it does for fruits and vegetables.

Incursions Against Liberty

Unfortunately, the world is full of busybodies and scolds seeking to expand the power of government by intruding into private and personal decisions about what people can eat. That is why they require restaurants to provide caloric information about everything they serve and seek to restrict fast-food establishments. It is why, in general, they treat us like children or fools who cannot be allowed to decide what we eat, how much we eat, and where we eat.

Beef production has nothing to do with global warming because there is no significant human-induced global warming. What warming occurred after the Little Ice Age ended in 1850 has been natural. So-called "greenhouse gas emissions"—from animals, humans, or energy use—have no impact on the climate.

For that you need to look to the sun, the oceans, clouds, volcanic eruptions, and events well beyond human control.

Hungry? Have a steak. Have a hamburger. Have some ribs. Eat some meat! The Earth will be just fine, and so will you.

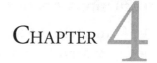

CHAPTER 4

What Is the Future for Vegetarianism?

Chapter Preface

Since 1900, the world has experienced the largest population growth in human history—a gain of more than 5 billion people in a little more than a century. Today, the global population stands at 6.8 billion people, but according to the United Nations the world will add another 2.4 billion people over the next 40 years, growing the global population to a burgeoning 9.2 billion by 2050. Thanks largely to immigration, the United States alone will add about 100 million people to its population by mid-century, increasing the U.S. population from 306 million to more than 400 million. Most of the current global population growth, however, is concentrated in developing countries. Some experts think that the human population is already too large to be environmentally sustainable—the threshold at which humans can use resources without depleting the environment—and many question how the world will feed even more people in the decades ahead.

The twentieth century's population boom has often been attributed to changes brought by the Industrial Revolution—the massive social and economic transformation that began in the 1800s in Europe and the United States and that mechanized most forms of labor, bringing wealth and prosperity to many around the world. Most importantly, with respect to agriculture, the mechanization of farm equipment, the increasing use of fossil fuels, and the introduction of pesticides and fertilizers obtained from petrochemicals helped to create the Green Revolution—a transformation of agriculture that allowed food production to keep up with exploding world population growth. In fact, between 1950 and 1984, the world's farmers expanded grain production by 250 percent, helping to avoid widespread famine and providing food security to many developing nations.

Yet despite its success, the Green Revolution, according to most environmentalists, has been very costly to the environment. Green Revolution technologies spawned huge, corporate-owned agribusinesses that specialize in growing just a few types of crops over thousands of acres, destroying the natural biodiversity seen in traditional agriculture. Modern farmers also became reliant on using larger and larger quantities of toxic chemical pesticides and fertilizers, which have polluted the soil and contaminated ground water. Over time, many farmlands subjected to these modern farming techniques have become agriculturally unproductive, and around the world regions that were once fertile are experiencing problems, such as soil erosion, drought, and desertification (the transformation of arable land into desert). Industrial-style farming is also credited with contributing to global warming, and cropland expansion has been a major driver of deforestation in the tropics.

Given these environmental downsides, many commentators say it is foolhardy to believe that the world's farmers can engineer a second "green revolution" large enough to feed the growing global population. Even now, according to food policy experts, there are signs that agricultural production is not keeping up with the demand for food. One such sign is rising food prices. Between 2005 and 2008, the price of wheat and corn tripled, and the price of rice increased five-fold—price hikes that stretched consumer budgets in developed countries and produced food riots in the developing world. A global recession, which began in 2008, has helped to moderate food prices, but prices remain at record levels and are expected to increase again once the recession ends and demand rises. And experts say climate change, which is expected to produce hotter growing seasons and more droughts and water shortages, will further stress agricultural production in the future. As a result, many commentators are predicting a global food crisis, in which the world will not be able to produce enough food for all the human beings living on the planet.

The looming food crisis is made even worse by the fact that more and more people want to eat meat. As countries like China and India develop and become more prosperous, their demand for grain has spiked, not because they need grain to feed people, but because it is needed to feed animals to satisfy their growing appetite for meat. Indeed, because of the changing diet of people in rapidly developing countries, world meat consumption is expected to double by 2050. Of course, as grains are diverted to feeding livestock, there is even less food available to feed the world's poor, who otherwise would consume the grain harvests themselves.

Many agricultural scientists and agriculture companies are betting that the solution is biotechnology. With the new knowledge scientists have recently gained about plant genetics, companies like Monsanto, Novartis, AgrEvo, and DuPont hope to develop new varieties of staple crops, such as corn, cotton, and soybeans, that will produce higher yields, need less fertilizer, and be drought tolerant. Other agricultural experts, including the United Nations' Food and Agriculture Organization (FAO), say that genetically engineered seeds will simply continue the unsustainable path followed after the original Green Revolution, based on the same agricultural practices and requiring the same chemical and fossil fuel inputs. The FAO and experts from around the world have called instead for a major shift in agriculture toward more sustainable and ecologically friendly farming methods. Such a movement would focus on small-scale, biologically diverse farms that use natural compost and manure fertilizers and avoid or severely limit the use of fossil fuels and petro-chemicals. Smaller, more ecological farms, proponents claim, would not only be good for the environment and human health, they would also produce more food, and would bring greater prosperity to the world's 900 million small farmers.

Vegetarianism, advocates say, offers yet another possible solution for a future food crisis. Since it takes five to eight pounds of grain to make one pound of meat, vegetarians argue that cutting back on or eliminating meat from our diet is a simple and effective way to eat as efficiently as possible, providing more food for everyone else. The authors in this chapter address the problem of future food production and the future of vegetarianism.

Vegetarianism Will Increase
in Years to Come

Heather Gorn

Heather Gorn is a researcher and writer for Vegetarian Journal, *a magazine devoted to vegetariansim.*

For this special 25th anniversary issue of *Vegetarian Journal*, I could think of nothing more appropriate than reflecting on the changing state of vegetarianism over the past quarter of a century. I asked a number of prominent activists to help with this project. These are some of the people who have been involved in promoting vegetarianism for 25 years or more. With their unique and experienced perspectives, I took a look back at this country's rediscovery of vegetarianism in the 1960s and 1970s, a look at vegetarianism in the present, and a look into the future. Thank you to everyone who shared their thoughts with us on this special occasion. We look forward to the next 25 years!

Frances Moore Lappe, Author of *Diet for a Small Planet*

I grew up in Texas, so the idea of surviving without meat was considered utterly unthinkable. The dominant paradigm was that you could not be healthy without meat and that meat was the center of a healthy diet—meat is what made you strong and smart. I remember this advertisement that I referenced in an early edition of *Diet for a Small Planet*. There was a picture of filet mignon and it said, "This is what you serve if you want to impress your brother-in-law." Meat was what you ate to impress people as well as what you ate just to live and be strong.

Heather Gorn, "25 Years of Vegetarianism and a Look into the Future," *Vegetarian Journal*, July 1, 2007. Reproduced by permission of The Vegetarian Resource Group, www.vrg.org.

I remember the early readers of *Diet for a Small Planet*, the young people who became vegetarian and their parents were terrified that they would die! And I remember joking with people that one of the most important things that my book did was relieve worried parents who thought their children were going to get sick and die without meat. People could not imagine a meal without meat. The meal was centered around the meat in the middle, and then you had your starch and your veggie, and that's what the meal was. To start to think of the meal in a different way is huge, and that's what I tried to do with the recipes in *Diet for a Small Planet*, to organize them in types of meals where you had different things in the center.

I thought *Diet for a Small Planet* was going to appeal to 500 people in the San Francisco Bay area, and I was going to publish it myself. When a New York publisher was interested and then it started to sell, I realized that there were millions of people looking for a way to have meaning in their everyday choices. It is so powerful that, in a world where people feel so powerless, they can feel that everyday choices, in choices that people make several times a day, ripple out and affect the earth and affect other people. I think that it was so cool for people to realize that every time they eat in the plant world, they are voting for a shift away from this very wasteful, destructive, and cruel system. It's something that's so moving, and so easy to do.

Now, we have knowledge about the danger of a meat-centered diet. That was brand new 25 years ago. When I was growing up, no one knew the research about heart disease related to saturated fats. And it has gone hand-in-hand with the environmental movement. When I wrote *Diet for a Small Planet*, the word 'ecology' had just barely reached its first birthday, so the fact that food had something to do with ecology and the environment was a brand new idea. People were beginning to think about the impact of their food consumption, and I think a lot of people were really moved to say, "Wait a minute, why do I need to eat a wasteful diet when I can eat one that is so good for me and the planet?" It's a win-win-win why not? And when I opened my eyes to the plant world, I realized that this was where the variety was—in texture, color, shape, and taste; there are endless possibilities. I think that is part of embracing other cuisines—it has allowed everyone to open up to all dimensions of a plant-centered diet and all the kinds of foods that you can create.

I have never felt comfortable predicting the future, but what I've seen in the past few years is books like Center for Science in the Public Interest's new book, *Six Arguments for a Greener Diet*; I feel like it's come full circle. A new generation is discovering all of these reasons that are still powerful today. I think that the interest going forward is going to go a lot from ecological awareness and people like the Union of Concerned Scientists saying, "Yeah, you can get a Prius [Toyota's hybrid electric car], but maybe just as important is eating low on the food chain," and people awakening to the fact that not eating meat is just as important as not driving a gas-guzzling car, or maybe more so. There is still a growing interest in animal cruelty—a motivation to relieve animal suffering—and I'm sure that will continue. But I think that equally strong and stronger will be the environmental impetus as people realize that we just can't tolerate this kind of waste.

Seth Tibbott, Inventor of Tofurky and Owner of Turtle Island Foods

I first became a vegetarian in college. The year was 1973, and my first vegetarian meal was a bowl of lentils, rice, and onions from Frances Moore Lappe's classic *Diet for a Small Planet*. I was a teacher/naturalist in training so the environmental aspect of Lappe's book appealed to me. It just made sense that eating plants directly was smarter, more efficient, and better on our battered ecosystems. My mom was unimpressed. She grew up during the Depression and to her it all came down to protein. How was I going to get my protein, she would ask, whenever I called home from Ohio, where I was living. There were no natural foods stores then, but you could buy brightly colored rainbow bags of granola and yogurt, too, in the local head shop. Both items became a staple for me, along with boxes of vanilla wafers. Not a great diet but a start.

Flash forward to 1977 and I was working as a naturalist at outdoor schools in Oregon. My mom was still bugging me about protein, and the first rudimentary co-ops were forming in garages and old warehouses around Portland. I started buying soy grits and making them into soy burgers. Wandering the aisles of the supermarkets, I also was impressed to see entire shelves of yogurt and granola. I had been reading the books of Stephen Gaskin and his 1,700-acre farm in Tennessee. I believe they had over a thousand hippies living on The Farm, all of whom subsisted on a 'pure vegetarian' diet that was in reality vegan, but I never heard them use the word. They grew soybeans on The Farm and had sent people to the libraries of the National Institutes of Health in Washington, DC, to research how they could use all these soybeans. When I landed a naturalist job that summer in Tennessee on the banks of the Nolichucky River, I took a weekend visit to The Farm and brought back my first tempeh spores. My friends and I were living in tents then, but the weather was hot and humid, perfect for incubating tempeh in stainless steel pans outside. It was love at first bite, eating that first batch of tempeh on the banks of the Nolichucky with Silver Queen sweet corn and okara (soy pulp).

This is all background for 1980, which is when Turtle Island Soy Dairy was founded at Hope Co-op in Forest Grove, Oregon. Back then, the natural foods industry was in its infancy still. The dark, funky co-ops had moved out of the garages and some small stores like Natures in Portland were actually starting to buy new freezers and refrigerated cases.

When I brought my first tempeh to the natural foods stores in Portland, it was very easy to get placement for all my three flavors: Soy Tempeh, Five Grain Tempeh, and Tempehroni, a sausage-shaped log of tempeh fermented with herbs and spices. In fact, the people working in the store were like, "Hey, what took you so long to come here? Now we can fill up our empty shelves with something!"

Today, it's amazing to see the plethora of vegetarian products vying for shelf space in not only natural foods stores but grocery stores as well.

Acceptance from the public was slower and took a lot of education, demos, etc. In fact, during the '80s, soybeans did not really have a great reputation. There wasn't a lot of information (pre-Internet days here, so information traveled slowly, largely through collections of paper with words typed on them and bound together in something called 'books!') on the health benefits of soybeans and soyfoods in general. You could maybe buy tofu in a few enlightened supermarkets, but mostly water-packed tofu was only sold in natural foods stores. In the mid-80s the first Gardenburgers were produced and one of their big selling points was "soy free," which it said across the front of the box. This changed in the 1990s when more and more information became available about positive aspects of soybeans and vegetarian diets in general, culminating in the FDA [U.S. Food and Drug Administration] allowing manufacturers to make health claims about soy protein.

Today, it's amazing to see the plethora of vegetarian products vying for shelf space in not only natural foods stores but grocery stores as well. It is many, many times easier to eat a healthy vegetarian or vegan diet than 25 years ago. The products just keep evolving and getting better and better. In 1980 you pretty much had to make your own vegetarian meals from scratch by a process involving ovens and stoves quaintly called 'cooking.' Now you just need a good freezer and micro-wave, and your options for quick, delicious tasty meals are literally too numerous to count.

Vegetarianism has too much truth and innate sensibility going for it not to bubble into an increasingly larger part of the world's diet in the years to come.

Yet I am still puzzled by the strength of the meat industry and the fact that more about the staggering environmental and health impacts of carnivorous diets is not of greater concern. As I look forward, I believe that eventually these two issues will bubble up to the surface, pushing more and more people to change their diets. Something has got to give here. Best guess is that vegetarian foods will continue to improve in tastes and textures and gain larger and larger market share and acceptance. Meat raised from livestock may lose its dominant place in the American diet and may become an expensive 'delicacy' that only the rich can afford. I would imagine that some type of meat replacement (non-vegetarian) will be grown in labs on an industrial scale and compete with vegetarian meat replacements. This new synthetic meat may have some of the environmental/health concerns removed from it and actually will be marketed as an alternative to the vegetarian meat alternatives.

Evolution is a painstakingly slow process, but even though truth can be suppressed, spun, and twisted, eventually it all comes to the surface, and vegetarianism has too much truth and innate sensibility going for it not to bubble into an increasingly larger part of the world's diet in the years to come.

Laurel Robertson, Author
of *Laurel's Kitchen*

Today, everyone knows that vegetarian eating is healthier! But in 'those days,' doctors and mothers (and sometimes maybe even we) fretted that our lives would be short and decrepit. Hard to believe now but true! Before *Laurel's Kitchen* was published in 1976, you could not find any popular scientifically sound nutritional information, vegetarian or not. And forget about finding good vegetarian recipes or restaurants. There's been a vast improvement since then!

On the other side, you were not surrounded by junk food 25 years ago. Most people sat down to meals of mostly real food. Yes, bread was white, and yes, you'd enjoy the occasional birthday cake. But junk wasn't everywhere, wasn't anything like often. Ominously, we see junk burrowing deeper. More and more, in the next 25 years, we will need to ask, what is real food? Where is it coming from? Who can afford it? And, which carrot is vegetarian?

Certainly, the '60s generation didn't invent vegetarianism. It took off in the '70s and '80s because of its newly recognized cachet of healthfulness and the newly appreciated ecological benefits of eating lower on the food chain. These are still valid reasons to eat vegetarian. Vegetarian popularity is due for an upswing. It depends a lot on us. How do we present our cause? By serving as walking proof that vegetarian eating is satisfying. Do we believe and show that it's delicious, pretty, easy, cheap, healthful, fun, and kind to animals and that it saves the rainforest? What's not to like?

Jim Rosen, Founder, Fantastic World Foods

Today, the idea of eating vegetarian foods in the U.S. is much more common and acceptable to the general public than 25 years ago. In the '70s and '80s, it was a foreign idea to most people. Waiters in restaurants made funny faces when quizzed about ingredients. My children, who grew up as vegetarians, were teased in school. Today, they are respected for being vegetarian. Doctors in general did not advise their patients to avoid meat. Today, practically every doctor recommends cutting back. Twenty-five years ago, there were only a few companies like Fantastic Foods producing vegetarian foods, and the products were sold only in health foods stores. Today, vegetarian products are produced by large companies and comprise one of the fastest growing categories in supermarkets.

One day eating meat will be seen as decadent, cruel, and irresponsible.

Vegetarianism is a trend as opposed to a fad. While the number of true vegetarians is increasing slowly, a rapidly growing segment of consumers chooses to eat vegetarian meals on a regular basis. Meat consumption is down. Today, there is an animal protein glut in this country. Mad cow disease, cancer, arteriolosclerosis, mercury poisoning in fish, etc., have scared people into eating 'more vegetarian.'

In the future, our society (and others) will move to a more vegetarian diet. There are three good reasons why a person chooses to be a vegetarian: compassion/spiritual, health, and environment. In the first category, the number of people who really feel empathy for the suffering of animals is very small today; however, as we evolve into a more aware and enlightened state of mind, the numbers will grow. Second, the aging of the population is making us more aware of the effect of diet on our health. Though this group generally will not become pure vegetarians, they will eat less animal protein. Finally, with respect to the environment, it appears that, as a society, we are about to become very 'green.' Author Thomas Friedman recently wrote that 'green' is the next red, white, and blue. Over the next few years, we will see a powerful environmental movement. As it takes shape, it will be hard to ignore all the evidence that switching to a vegetarian diet could be the most environmentally responsible thing a person could do. One day eating meat will be seen as decadent, cruel, and irresponsible. Twenty-five years from now, I believe that vegetarianism will be the rule rather than the exception. . . .

Ingrid Newkirk, Co-Founder and President of People for the Ethical Treatment of Animals (PETA)

Cranks! That was the name of the London restaurant for vegetarians and our family's steamed 'Christmas puddings,' which contained a lucky coin and were made with fat from unlucky cows. We were a rare breed, walking our lonely walk through meaty and milky supermarket aisles, having 'given up' the foods we were raised on, whether steak and kidney pie and roast beef or hot dogs and hamburgers. "How bizarre!" said a waitress, when I explained my dietary preference.

Today, there are veggie burgers in every 'fish and chip' shop in England and vegan cuisine on the menu at Brown's and other lah-di-da places to eat, and there is not only vegan Christmas pudding but vegan haggis (blood sausage) and vegan 'caviar.' My local southern Virginia grocery has shelves creaking with soymilk, and there are faux chicken nuggets in the freezer case. We want for no sensation that our tastebuds once knew but our intellect and hearts rejected. The medical profession, writers, and even most of the carcass-crunching masses realize now that we vegans have not 'given up' anything except a bigger chance of experiencing heart disease and stroke.

I can't wait to read what we'll say in 25 more years! I see vegetarian ideals permeating the Muslim world via small beginnings such as the website, warning labels on meat and milk, the end of government subsidies for poisonous meat and dairy products, physicians telling patients (as they do now with smoking) to stay off animal protein, and new vegan adults, born of their enlightenment from growing up in vegan households and veganized school lunch lines.

Thanks to VRG's [The Vegetarian Resource Group] work and that of so many individuals who care about animals, human health, and more, being a daily ambassador for vegan living is no longer hard, pioneering work—it is a pleasant duty. Happy Anniversary, you wonderful people!

People Will Increasingly Boycott Factory-Farmed Meat and Animal Products

Nicolette Hahn Niman

Nicolette Hahn Niman is an environmental lawyer, writer, and author of the book Righteous Porkchop: Finding a Life and Good Food Beyond Factory Farms. *She lives in Bolinas, California, with her husband, Bill Niman, founder of Niman Ranch, a natural meat company.*

Most people share at least the following traits: they want to be healthy; they like animals; and they value clean air and water. Yet relatively few Americans connect those concerns with their food. As more people start making the link (especially if they've seen graphic video footage of industrial animal operations), many decide it's time to stop eating foods from factory farms. This is a guide for doing just that. . . .

General Advice

1. Be prepared to pay more. As the old saying goes, "you get what you pay for." Americans are used to the idea that a Cadillac is a better car than a Malibu and that you pay more for it. Yet somehow when it comes to food many of us look only at price. But getting good food could be one of the most important things we do to keep ourselves in good health. To paraphrase [food and environmental writer] Michael Pollan, you pay your grocer now or pay your doctor later. And the methods for producing foods—especially animal based foods—vary radically, from farms that are excellent stewards of animals and the environment to the most industrialized, stinking, polluting facilities. Instead of just looking at price

Nicolette Hahn Niman, "Avoiding Factory Farm Foods: An Eater's Guide," *The Huffington Post*, November 11, 2009. Reproduced by permission of the author.

tags, think in terms of value. Remember that our government heavily subsidizes industrial agriculture, making its products artificially cheap. We should all be asking our elected officials why our government isn't supporting farming that produces food that's healthful for humans, environmentally benign and respectful to animals. Over the long term, that's the change we need to advocate for. If government policy made such a shift, wholesome traditionally produced foods could be as inexpensive as the junk coming out of factory farms. In the meantime, expect to pay more for good food. Think of it as an investment in good health, an unspoiled environment, fair treatment for animals, and of course, tasty eating.

Consider adopting this as your new slogan: Eat less meat. Eat better meat.

---

2. Plan on reducing consumption. A typical American eats more than 200 pounds of meat per year and our consumption continues to rise. On top of that, over the twentieth century, average cheese consumption went from about three pounds annually to around 30 pounds, much of which is processed cheese in Big Macs and on pizzas. (And we wonder why we have an obesity epidemic). Meat and dairy products from traditional farms currently cost more than factory farm products. A good way to make this work in your budget is to cut back the quantities you buy (and the frequency and portion sizes when you eat animal based foods). Chances are, you're eating far more of it than you need anyway, so cutting back will probably be a good thing for your health as well. Consider adopting this as your new slogan: *Eat less meat. Eat better meat.* (The same goes for dairy products and eggs).

3. Seek food from a known source. The best way to ensure you're getting food from non-industrial farms is to buy from sources with full transparency, those where you can see how the animals are raised, and what they were fed, as well as learn from what farm or farms the food actually came. If I can't get the basic information about how the farm animals were raised, I just don't buy it.

4. Ask questions (even if it sometimes seems futile). Few people these days ask where the food comes from when at grocery stores or restaurants. Americans have become accustomed to the idea that there's some giant commodity trade of fungible meats, eggs, and dairy products. But there is real power in simply asking the questions: "Where is this from? How was it raised?" Get into the habit at meat counters and restaurants of asking where the meat is from. If they don't know the answer, suggest (in a friendly way, of course) they find out. When we eat out, Bill and I always ask servers where the meat comes from. If they don't know, we ask them to ask the chef. If the chef doesn't know, Bill doesn't order it. I believe the simple act of asking this question—if enough people begin to do it—has the potential to spark a massive change in our food system.

5. Know your labels (and their shortcomings). Food labels are helpful but imperfect. Knowing what they mean (and do not mean) is important. For example, the term "free range" has one connotation with eggs and another with poultry meat. Weird, huh? This is something you'd never know just by looking at the labels in the store. Most labeling is regulated by the Department of Agriculture (USDA), so they are fairly reliable sources of some information.

6. Baby-steps are OK (as long as they're in the right direction). Factory farms are ubiquitous and so are their products. So avoiding them, admittedly, takes some effort. If you try to change everything in one fell swoop you're likely to feel so overwhelmed that you'll get paralyzed and give up. If, on the other hand, you allow yourself to move forward deliberately, one step at a time, chances are you will enjoy the transition and will stick with it.

7. *Consider it an adventure.* Going to the supermarket to pick up all your food is convenient, true, but it's also dreadfully boring. Good foods from real farms do not look and taste the same 365 days a year. They are less predictable, varying depending on the particular breeds of animal, the seasons, and the farmer who raised them. The diversity of the foods you'll get from real farms is just part of what makes eating more fun. It's also a pleasure to meet and talk with farmers, butchers and other purveyors of real foods. They can be tremendously helpful in providing cooking advice for the particular foods you are buying (such as a cut of meat you've never tried). Following the pathways that lead you to good foods—farmstands, CSAs [Community Supported Agriculture], farmers markets, co-ops—will take you to interesting places you've never been and to people you'll enjoy meeting.

Where to Look

1. *Stop being a supermarket zombie.* Supermarkets' primary appeal is convenience, and there's no doubt that they are convenient. They are also offering more organic foods these days, which is a good thing. But because their business model is based on large volumes of uniform products, supermarkets rarely carry foods from real, traditional family farms. In my experience, places like Safeway, Albertsons, and Kroger are wastelands for those of us seeking animal products that don't come from factory farms. That's why (other than Trader Joes and Whole Foods, which are better than the rest) I have almost totally stopped frequenting them. The exception to this general rule is for those farms who've joined together to cooperatively process and distribute their products, thus they have sufficient volume to work with major supermarket chains.

2. *Explore alternative stores (independent grocery stores and co-ops).* Independently owned grocery stores tend to be more willing to work with traditional farmers, and their staffs are generally much more knowledgeable about the meats, eggs

and dairy products they offer. It's worth the effort to seek them out and explore their offerings. Good examples of such stores are: Bi-Rite Market in San Francisco; Marczyk Fine Foods in Denver; Gateway Market in Des Moines; and Poppies Gourmet Farmers Market in Brevard, North Carolina. Co-ops also tend to source from local farmers and have member-employees who are interested and concerned about good food. Examples of some of the excellent co-ops I'm familiar with are: the co-ops in Boise, Idaho and Bozeman, Montana, and "The Wedge" in Minneapolis.

Organic is very good (but the label isn't perfect).

---

3. Frequent your local farmers markets. The popularity of farmers markets has exploded in recent past decades, going from about 350 in the late 1970s to more than 4,400 today. This is excellent news for those of us seeking non-factory farm foods. With a little effort, you can find a farmers market near you and begin learning what's offered there at what times of year. Many excellent farms and ranches sell their wares at farmers markets but remember not to assume anything about how the foods were produced. Ask the farmers you're buying from how the animals were raised and what they were fed. Locating a farmers market is easy: many states and localities have lists available, as does USDA.

4. Look for CSAs. An excellent way to know exactly where your food comes from is to join a CSA (community supported agriculture). You buy shares of what a farm produces. Generally, each "shareholder" (member) gets a box of farm products each week, which members pick up at a certain spot. Many CSAs encourage their shareholders to visit the farms for themselves, so they can really know where their food is coming from and how it was raised. When they first started, most CSAs were just doing produce. But in recent years, I've spoken with people from all over the country that are doing CSAs that include meat, dairy and eggs. Some farms and ranches are even doing CSAs that are exclusively animal-based foods. CSAs can be found by searching Eatwellguide.org and Localharvest.org/csa.

5. *Look for farms online.* Many smaller farms and ranches sell directly to consumers with a website. The other day, for example, I was speaking at a Sierra Club conference in Kentucky and met a local farmer who's raising Bourbon Red heritage turkeys. She told me she [sells] most of her birds through her on-line store. Be sure that the website provides plenty of photos and information about how they raise their animals. If it's just showing photos of the food products, that's a bad sign.

6. *Seek chefs committed to sustainable sourcing.* It can be especially hard to trace the origins of your food when dining out. However, if you seek restaurants whose chefs are dedicated to sourcing from sustainable farms and ranches, they can do the work for you. Fortunately, the number of such restaurants is growing. Here are just a few of my favorites: Lumiere, near Boston; Savoy and Green Table in New York City; White Dog Café in Philadelphia; North Pond in Chicago; Zingermann's in Ann Arbor, MI; Highlands Bar and Grill in Birmingham, AL; Chez Panisse in Berkeley, CA; and Oliveto in Oakland, CA. An organization that promotes sustainable sourcing to chefs (and on whose board I sit), Chefs Collaborative, has a website listing of participating restaurants throughout the country which buy all or some of their ingredients from sustainable farms. Another good way to find such restaurants is Eatwellguide.org. Even fast food is possible: Chipotle Mexican Grills buy all their pork from traditional farms.

What to Look for with All Animal Based Foods

1. *Domestic, please.* Whether you're worried about your food's carbon footprint or how much you can verify about its source, there are lots of good reasons to support farms close to home.

I am generally skeptical about claims (like "organic") on food imported from foreign countries. US government authorities barely police imported food's safety nor the validity of its label claims. We always try to buy domestically because we want to feel confident about how it was produced. We also want to help build the demand for traditionally farmed foods so that more and more American farmland is occupied by real farms and ranches instead of factory farms. Of course, when you're shopping at a farmers market, this is generally not a concern. But lots of stores offer imported meats and fish. In particular, 90 percent of lamb comes from Australia and New Zealand and most seafood comes from Asia.

2. Pasture is the gold standard. All animals, not just grazing animals, benefit tremendously from being outdoors daily on natural vegetation (such as grass and clover). They exercise, lie in the sun, breathe fresh air, and generally live much happier, healthier, more natural lives. For cattle, sheep, and goats, their ruminant digestive systems miraculously turn vegetation that is inedible to humans into digestible nourishment for themselves. The omnivorous animals—pigs, chickens, and turkeys—gain minerals and fiber from their foraging. Winter weather makes year-round access to pasture difficult in some parts of the United States, but animals can and should have access to grass for most days of the year. They live healthier, better lives and the food humans take from them is safer, tastier and healthier. If you're buying directly from a farmer or rancher, ask if the animals were on pasture. If you're buying from a store, read the labels or ask. If it doesn't say the animals had pasture access, assume that they did not.

3. Grass fed is very good (but the label is weak). Certain animals, including cattle, goats and sheep, have evolved as grazing or browsing animals. Their bodies are designed to spend their waking hours slowly foraging and walking to gather their food over many hours. Bovines in the wild, for instance, spend most of their waking hours in a state of slow, ambulant grazing, walking an average of 2.5 miles a day, all the while taking 50 to 80 bites of forage per minute. In other words, cattle—both those raised for beef and those raised for milk—should live on grass. In 2007, USDA finally proposed a standard for "grass fed" meat. However, the standard has lots of problems, not the least of which is that it doesn't require animals to be on pasture and allows them to be fed lots of stuff that definitely ain't grass. That's why it's preferable to buy grass fed meat directly from the farmer or rancher rather than relying on a label.

2. *Organic is very good (but the label isn't perfect).* USDA regulates the use of the term "organic" on food labels. If you see the official "Certified Organic" label on a food, that means that USDA is maintaining a certain degree of oversight and that the food item was (or at least should have been) produced in accordance with USDA's standards. In many ways, especially with respect to animal feeding, the standards are stringent. Animal based foods labeled organic must be fed only organic feeds (which has at least 80 percent organic ingredients and does not contain slaughterhouse wastes, antibiotics, or genetically modified grains). These are important distinctions from typical factory farm foods. The organic standards also provide some assurance about how the animals are housed and handled. They require that organic livestock and poultry be provided: "living conditions which accommodate the health and natural behavior of animals," and specifically mandate that animals have some access to the outdoors, to exercise, and to bedding. These too are crucial differences from factory farms. The problem, however, is that the standards have not clearly mandated access to pasture. Thus, much organic milk (and other dairy products) comes from cows that are housed in enormous metal sheds and spend most of their days on cement floors, having no access to pastures. For this reason, I prefer to know precisely where and how the animals lived that produced my food and do not like to rely on the organic label.

3. Free range is okay (but the label is seriously flawed). The term "free range" is most commonly used for poultry. Strangely, it can mean different things depending on whether it's applied to poultry raised for meat versus egg-laying poultry. When "free range" is used on poultry meat, USDA requires that the birds have some access to the outdoors. However, there are no standards for what type of outdoor area it must be, and therefore might be a small cement patio. Even more problematic is "free range" when it's used for eggs. USDA has failed to create any definition of "free range" for egg laying hens. Arguably, then, companies could label their eggs "free range" even without providing any outdoor access (and I suspect that's what some companies are doing).

4. Antibiotic free doesn't mean much. Some poultry and red meats are labeled "antibiotic free." This is slightly better than your average factory farm product because the animals were not continually fed antibiotics. But there are several serious problems with this label. Most importantly, "antibiotic free" meat can be (and usually is) from a factory farm. Secondly, many companies are calling meat antibiotic free even though they used other anti-microbial drugs to raise the animals. In other words, it's largely a matter of semantics.

Lab-Grown Meat Will Positively Impact the Planet

Hank Hyena

Hank Hyena is a comedian, writer, and journalist who has written for many different magazines and online publications.

"Future Flesh" is squatting on your plate. Are you nervous? Stab it with a fork. Sniff it. Bite! Chew, swallow. Congratulations! Relax and ruminate now because you're digesting a muscular invention that will massively impact the planet.

In-Vitro Meat—aka tank steak, sci fi sausage, petri pork, beaker bacon, Frankenburger, vat-grown veal, laboratory lamb, synthetic shmeat, trans-ham, factory filet, test tube tuna, cultured chicken, or any other moniker that can seduce the shopper's stomach—will appear in 3–10 years as a cheaper, healthier, "greener" protein that's easily manufactured in a metropolis. Its entree will be enormous; not just food-huge like curry rippling through London in the 1970's or colonized tomatoes teaming up with pasta in early 1800's Italy. No. Bigger. In-Vitro Meat will be socially transformative, like automobiles, cinema, vaccines.

H+ [magazine] previously discussed In-Vitro Meat, as have numerous other publications. Science pundits examined its microbiological struggles in Dutch labs and at New Harvest, a Baltimore non-profit. Squeamish reporters wasted ink on its "yucky" and "unnatural" creation, while others wondered if its "vegan" or not (PETA [People for the Ethical Treatment of Animals] supports it but many members complain). This article jumps past artificial tissue issues; anticipating success, I optimistically envision Eight Ways In-Vitro Meat Will Change Our Lives.

1. Bye-Bye Ranches. When In-Vitro Meat (IVM) is cheaper than meat-on-the-hoof-or-claw, no one will buy the undercut opponent. Slow-grown red meat & poultry will vanish from the marketplace, similar to whale oil's flame out when kerosene outshone it in the 1870's. Predictors believe that IVM will sell for half the cost of its murdered rivals. This will grind the $2 trillion global live-meat industry to a halt (500 billion pounds of meat are gobbled annually; this is expected to double by 2050). Bloody sentimentality will keep the slaughterhouses briefly busy as ranchers quick-kill their inventory before it becomes worthless, but soon Wall Street will be awash in unwanted pork bellies.

Slow-grown red meat & poultry will vanish from the marketplace.

Special Note: IVM sales will be aided by continued outbreaks of filthy over-crowded farm animal diseases like swine flu, Mad Cow, avian flu, tuberculosis [TB], brucellosis, and other animal-to-human plagues. Public hysteria will demand pre-emptive annihilation of the enormous herds and flocks where deadly pathogens form, after safe IVM protein is available.

2. Urban Cowboys. Today's gentle drift into urbanization will suddenly accelerate as unemployed livestock workers relocate and retrain for city occupations. Rural real estate values will plummet as vast tracts of ranch land are abandoned and sold for a pittance (70% of arable land in the world is currently used for livestock, 26% of the total land surface, according to the United Nations Food and Agriculture Organization). New use for ex-ranch land? Inexpensive vacation homes; reforested parks; fields of green products like hemp or bamboo. Hot new city job? Techies and designers for In-Vitro Meat factories.

3. *Healthier Humans.* In-Vitro Meat will be 100% muscle. It will eliminate the artery-clogging saturated fat that kills us. Instead, heart-healthy Omega-3 (salmon oil) will be added. IVM will also contain no hormones, salmonella, e. coli, campylobacter, mercury, dioxin, or antibiotics that infect primitive meat. I've noted above that IVM will reduce influenza, brucellosis, TB, and Mad Cow Disease. Starvation and kwashiokor (protein deficiency) will be conquered when compact IVM kits are delivered to famine-plagued nations. The globe's water crises will be partially alleviated, due to our inheritance of the 8% of the H2O [water] supply that was previously gulped down by livestock and their food crops. We won't even choke to death because IVM contains no malicious bones or gristle. . . .

4. *Healthier Planet.* A recent Worldwatch Institute report ("Livestock and Climate Change") accuses the world's 1.5 billion livestock of responsibility for 51% of all human-caused greenhouse gas emissions. Statistics are truly shitty: cattle crap 130 times more volume than a human, creating 64 million tons of sewage in the United States that's often flushed down the Mississippi River to kill fish and coral in the Gulf of Mexico. Pigs are equally putrid. There's a hog farm in Utah that oozes a bigger turd total than the entire city of Los Angeles. Livestock burps and farts are equally odious and ozone-destroying. 68% of the ammonia in the world is caused by livestock (creating acid rain), 65% of the nitrous oxide, 37% of the methane, 9% of the CO2 [carbon dioxide], plus 100 other polluting gases. Big meat animals waste valuable land— 80% of Amazon deforestation is for beef ranching, clear-cutting a Belgium-sized patch every year. Water is prodigiously gulped—15,000 liters of H2O produces just one kilogram of beef. 40% of the world's cereals are devoured by livestock. This scenario is clearly unsustainable, and In-Vitro Meat is the sensible alternative. (Although skeptics warn that IVM factories will produce their own emissions, research indicates that

pollution will be reduced by at least 80%.) Once we get over the fact that IVM is oddly disembodied, we'll be thankful that it doesn't shit, burp, fart, eat, over graze, drink, bleed, or scream in pain.

5. *Economic Upheaval.* The switch to In-Vitro Meat will pummel the finances of nations that survive on live animal industries. Many of the world leaders in massacred meat (USA, China, Brazil) have diversified incomes, but Argentina will bellow when its delicious beef is defeated. New Zealand will bleat when its lamb sales are shorn. And ocean-harvesting Vietnam and Iceland will have to fish for new vocations. Industries peripherally dependent on meat sales, like leather, dairy and wool, will also be slaughtered. Hide and leather-exporting nations like Pakistan and Kenya will be whipped, but South Korea will profit on its sales of "Koskin" and other synthetic leathers. Huge plantations of livestock crops (soybeans & corn) in Brazil, USA, Argentina, and China can be replaced with wool substitutes like sisal. Smaller nations that excel in food processing will thrive because they'll export IVM instead of importing tonnage of frozen meat. Look for economic upticks in The Netherlands, Belgium, Denmark, France, and especially Japan, who's currently one of the globe's largest importers of beef.

6. *Exotic & Kinky Cuisine.* In-Vitro Meat will be fashioned from any creature, not just domestics that were affordable to farm. Yes, ANY ANIMAL, even rare beasts like snow leopard, or Komodo Dragon. We will want to taste them all. Some researchers believe we will also be able to create IVM using the DNA of extinct beasts—obviously, "DinoBurgers" will be served at every six-year-old boy's birthday party.

Humans are animals, so every hipster will try Cannibalism. Perhaps we'll just eat people we don't like, as author Iain M. Banks predicted in his short story, "The State of the Art" with diners feasting on "Stewed Idi Amin." But I imagine passionate lovers literally eating each other, growing sausages from their co-mingled tissues overnight in tabletop appliances similar to bread-making machines. And of course, masturbatory gourmands will simply gobble their own meat.

7. FarmScrapers. The convenience of buying In-Vitro Meat fresh from the neighborhood factory will inspire urbanites to demand local vegetables and fruits. This will be accomplished with "vertical farming"—building gigantic urban multi-level greenhouses that utilize hydroponics and Interior grow-lights to create bug-free, dirt-free, quick-growing super veggies and fruit (from dwarf trees), delicious side dishes with IVM. No longer will old food arrive via long polluting transports from the hinterlands. Every metro dweller will purchase fresh meat and crispy plants within walking distance. The success of FarmScrapers will cripple rural agriculture and enhance urbanization.

8. We Stop the Shame. In-Vitro Meat will squelch the subliminal guilt that sensitive people feel when they sit down for a carnivorous meal. Forty billion animals are killed per year in the United States alone; one million chickens per hour. I list this last even though it's the top priority for vegetarians, because they represent only 1–2% of the population, but still. . . . IVM is a huge step forward in "Abolitionism"—the elimination of suffering in all sentient creatures. Peter Singer, founding father of Animal Liberation, supports IVM. So does every European veggie group I contacted: VEBU (Vegetarian Federation of Germany), EVA (Ethical Vegetarian Alternative of Belgium), and the Dutch Vegetarian Society. And PETA, mentioned earlier, offers $1 million to anyone who can market a competitive IVM product by 2012.

My final prediction is this: In-Vitro Meat relishes success first in Europe, partly because its "greener," but mostly they already eat "yucky" delicacies like snails, smoked eel, blood pudding, pig's head cheese, and haggis (sheep's stomach stuffed with oatmeal). In the USA, IVM will initially invade the market in Spam cans and Hot Dogs, shapes that salivating shoppers are sold on as mysterious & artificial, but edible & absolutely American.

Lab-Grown Meat Will Not Be Widespread in the Near Future

Brendan I. Koerner

Brendan I. Koerner is an author and a contributing editor at Wired, *a print and online magazine that provides in-depth coverage of current and future trends in technology and modern culture.*

It's easy to understand why the animal-rights set is so keen on lab-grown meat—no more slaughterhouses or veal pens. But should environmentalists be getting on the bandwagon, too? I'm always hearing how cow burps are a major contributor to global warming. Then again, those massive meat labs will require a lot of power, right?

The hypothetical meat labs won't be carbon-neutral, but they'll still be far greener than our current system for producing burgers and chops. Raising and slaughtering livestock on a large scale doesn't just result in massive methane emissions due to bovine flatulence; it also creates waste-disposal nightmares, squanders valuable land, and guzzles an alarming amount of fossil fuel. So, yes, the environmentally conscious should keep their fingers crossed that lab-grown meat becomes a reality sooner rather than later. But given the numerous scientific challenges that remain, they shouldn't get their hopes up.

The Benefits of Lab-Grown Meat

For the record, the Lantern [a blogger at Slate.com] is by no means averse to feasting on steak, chicken, or currywurst and has previously suggested that omnivorousness needn't be a mortal environmental sin. But he also acknowledges that our collective yen for meat, particularly cut-rate beef and pork, is taking its toll on the planet. According to a study published in *Animal Science Journal* last August, creating a pound's worth of beef releases the same amount of greenhouses gases—the equivalent of 36.4 pounds of carbon dioxide—as driving a car 155 miles at 50 miles per hour. And that's an underestimate of the industry's total impact, since the study didn't account for emissions from farm equipment or the fuel expended on transporting product from killing floor to supermarket.

Despite considerable hubbub over the technology in recent months, we're still years—or, more likely, decades—away from affordable lab-grown meat.

Making meat in the lab would eliminate not only the methane generated by belching cattle, but also the need to grow mass quantities of feed—a woefully inefficient use of land, given that a cow must consume seven calories of grain in order to produce a single calorie of beef. And once you factor in the petroleum required to raise that grain—a process that involves the use of synthetic fertilizers, among other environmental bogeymen—the ratio of input calories to output zooms to 35 to 1.

The energy requirements of laboratories, by contrast, pale in comparison. According to most proposals, tomorrow's beef would be grown in bioreactors, filled with a solution consisting primarily of water and glucose. Animal stem cells would be placed in these bioreactors, where their proliferation would be abetted by the presence of growth factors, perhaps made from fungi.

Relatively small amounts of electricity (potentially derived from solar panels) would be required to regulate the temperature in these bioreactors, but also to provide a bit of stimulation to the cells as they grow into tissues. To replicate the taste and mouth-feel of naturally grown meat, the lab-grown victuals would have to be exercised—cows stretch their muscle tissues when they move, which in turn affects the flavor of their flesh. A minor electric current can mimic the effects of bovine movement. There has also been talk of adding polysaccharide beads to the bioreactors; as the temperature or acidity of the solution changes, these beads would expand or contract, thus providing the necessary workout for the nascent tissue. The beads would likely be made from the exoskeletons of arthropods and are completely nontoxic.

Lab-grown meat would also be more efficient in that no energy would have to be expended to create unwanted byproducts—specifically skeletons. Nor would there be any problems with waste management, a big plus since manure is a worrying contaminant of water supplies. And the lab approach would make locavorism that much easier; why buy lamb cubes from 1,000 miles away when they can come from the corner bioreactor instead?

Our meat addiction is one of those environmental problems that we can't just invent ourselves out of.

Problems with Lab-Grown Meat

A lovely thought, but don't hold your breath while waiting for your first lab-grown roast. Despite considerable hubbub over the technology in recent months, we're still years—or, more likely, decades—away from affordable lab-grown meat. The current experiments are taking place in bioreactors that measure only a few hundred milliliters in volume, and the longest complete muscle tissues are just 2 centimeters long. Researchers are nowhere close to scaling up their production to market-ready levels, to say nothing of market-ready prices. A Dutch team's lab-grown pork, for example, would cost around

$45,000 per pound—assuming they could make an entire pound of the stuff. Bioreactors may be energy-efficient when compared with cattle, but they're also expensive to design, build, and maintain. They also require highly skilled personnel to manage, in order to preserve aseptic conditions.

Furthermore, manufactured meat promises to replicate only the taste and texture of processed meat; as far as we are from enjoying lab-grown hamburger, we're even further from perfecting manmade rib-eyes. So even if meat labs did become viable commercial enterprises, the naturally raised meat industry would hardly vanish.

Given our penchant for gluttony, affordable lab-grown meat could even be harmful to our health: We might simply increase our beef and pork consumption to keep pace with production, as has occurred over the past half-century. (According to this disturbing assessment, we annually consume 50 pounds more meat per-capita than Americans did in the 1950s.)

So while we should welcome the advent of lab-grown meat, we should also realize that it can't provide a short-term fix. Unfortunately, our meat addiction is one of those environmental problems that we can't just invent ourselves out of.

Meat-Eaters Should Be Taxed to Reduce Meat Consumption

Peter Singer

Peter Singer is a professor of bioethics at Princeton University, a well-known animal rights advocate, and a co-author of the book The Way We Eat: Why Our Food Choices Matter.

Taxes can do a lot of good. They pay for schools, parks, police and the military. But that's not all they can do. High taxes on cigarettes have saved many lives—not only the lives of people who are discouraged from smoking as much as they would if cigarettes were cheap, but also the lives of others who spend less time passively inhaling smoke.

No reasonable person would want to abolish the tax on cigarettes. Unless, perhaps, they were proposing banning cigarettes altogether—as New York City is doing with transfats served by restaurants.

A tax on sodas containing sugar has also been under consideration, by [New York] Governor [David] Paterson among others. In view of our obesity epidemic, and the extra burden it places on our health care system—not to mention the problems it causes on a crowded New York subway when your neighbor can't fit into a single seat—it's a reasonable proposal.

But in all these moves against tobacco, transfats and sodas, we've been ignoring the cow in the room.

That's right, cow. We don't eat elephants. But the reasons for a tax on beef and other meats are stronger than those for discouraging consumption of cigarettes, transfats or sugary drinks.

The Evils of Meat

First, eating red meat is likely to kill you. Large studies have shown that the daily consumption of red meat increases the risk that you will die prematurely of heart disease or bowel cancer. This is now beyond serious scientific dispute. When the beef industry tries to deny the evidence, it is just repeating what the tobacco industry did 30 years ago.

Second, we have laws that ban cruelty to animals. Unfortunately in the states in which most animals are raised for meat, the agribusiness lobby is so powerful that it has carved out exemptions to the usual laws against cruelty.

The exemptions allow producers to crowd chickens, pigs and calves in stinking sheds, never letting them go outside in fresh air and sunlight, often confining them so closely that they can't even stretch their limbs or turn around. De-beaking—cutting through the sensitive beak of a young chick with a hot blade—is standard in the egg industry.

Undercover investigations repeatedly turn up new scandals—downed cows being dragged to slaughter, workers hitting pigs with steel pipes or playing football with live chickens. We may not be able to improve the laws in those farming states, but taxes on meat would discourage people from supporting these cruel practices.

Taxing meat would be a highly effective way of reducing our greenhouse gas emissions and avoiding catastrophic climate change.

Third, industrial meat production wastes food—we feed the animals vast quantities of grains and soybeans, and they burn up most of the nutritional value of these crops just living and breathing and developing bones and other unpalatable body parts. We get back only a fraction of the food value we put into them.

That puts unnecessary pressure on our croplands and causes food prices to rise all over the world. Converting corn to biofuel has been criticized because it raises food prices for the world's poor, but seven times as much grain gets fed to animals as is made into biofuel.

Fourth, agricultural runoff—much of it from livestock production, or from the fertilizers used to grow the grain fed to the livestock—is the biggest single source of pollution of the nation's rivers and streams, according to the EPA [U.S. Environmental Protection Agency]. A meat tax would be an important step towards cleaner rivers. By reducing the amount of nitrogen that runs off fields in the Midwest into the Mississippi [River], it would also stop the vast "dead zone" that forms in the Gulf of Mexico each year.

Meat-eaters impose costs on others, and the more meat they eat, the greater the costs.

Meat and Global Warming

The clincher is that taxing meat would be a highly effective way of reducing our greenhouse gas emissions and avoiding catastrophic climate change.

Here's just how bad eating meat is for global warming.

Many people think that buying locally produced food is a good way to reduce their carbon footprint. But the average American would do more for the planet by going vegetarian just one day per week than by switching to a totally local diet.

In 2006 the United Nations Food and Agriculture Organization [FAO] surprised many people when it produced a report showing that livestock are responsible for more emissions than all forms of transportation combined. It's now clear that that report seriously underestimated the contribution that livestock—especially ruminant animals like cattle and sheep—are making to global warming.

As a more recent report by the Intergovernmental Panel on Climate Change has shown, over the critical next 20 years, the methane these animals produce will be almost three times as potent in warming the planet as the FAO report assumed.

Meat-eaters impose costs on others, and the more meat they eat, the greater the costs.

They push up our health insurance premiums, increase Medicare and Medicaid costs for taxpayers, pollute our rivers, threaten the survival of fishing communities in the Gulf of Mexico, push up food prices for the world's poor, and accelerate climate change.

Red meat is the worst for global warming, but a tax on red meat alone would merely push meat-eaters to chicken, and British animal welfare expert Professor John Webster has described the intensive chicken industry as "the single most severe, systematic example of man's inhumanity to another sentient animal."

So let's start with a 50% tax on the retail value of all meat, and see what difference that makes to present consumption habits. If it is not enough to bring about the change we need, then, like cigarette taxes, it will need to go higher.

Sustainable Meat Production and Reduced Consumption Can Feed the World

Collin Dunn

Collin Dunn is a sustainability enthusiast from Oregon who writes for TreeHugger *and* Planet Green, *Web magazines that focus on environmental issues.*

You don't have to be a vegetarian to eat green. Not only that, we can feed the fast-growing population of the planet, *and* slow down (and eventually stop) climate change, *and* stop destruction of the world's forests, all without the deleterious effects of factory farming.

So says a new [2009] report from Friends of the Earth, which lays out a model for food production and consumption that includes fair, healthy diets for the entire planet's population, and sustainable management of the planet's resources, too.

Sounds pretty good. But is it too good to be true?

The research models future food production with different farming methods, land use, and diets—72 different scenarios in all—and concludes that ample food can be produced for the global population that is expected to top nine billion by 2050. Doing so, however, will require a significant change from the intensive methods practiced by factory farms, and a more even distribution of calories across the population. In short: Everything in moderation.

A diet equivalent to eating meat three times a week would allow for sustainable land use—no need for more Amazon deforestation, for example—as well as for enough pasture for free-ranging livestock, and acreage to grow crops without extensive use of GMOs [genetically modified organisms], pesticides, and other industrial farming methods.

Changing the Factory Farming Paradigm

These conditions—enough food, enough land, sustainable methods all around—requires a variety of changes in the way we interact with food; for us in the developed world, the two biggies are carefully, sustainably sourcing it (to help continue building the infrastructure needed to produce it all—supply and demand), and doing so in moderation. Eating a bit of meat—something like a weekday vegetarian diet—is okay, so long as it doesn't come from the industrial agriculture complex and a factory farm.

A diet equivalent to eating meat three times a week would allow for sustainable land use . . . as well as for enough pasture for free-ranging livestock.

That isn't going to reduce the energy and inputs necessary to produce intensive products like beef and dairy; eating meat and drinking milk will continue to have a higher footprint than more vegetable-focused foods. But, with as many people obese in the developed world as malnourished in the developing world—about a billion each—the whole planet can stand to benefit from a more even distribution of calories and protein.

Lasse Bruun, Head of Campaigns at Compassion in World Farming, summed it up pretty succinctly, saying, "Animals are being reared like factory units to provide us with cheap meat. The true cost of eating too much meat is animal suffering, deforestation and obesity. We have the power to save our planet and be kind to animals. All we need to do is change our diets to a healthier and fairer option."

Balancing Food Production with Other Planetary Needs, Like Fuel

Doing so will require a more delicate balance of land use, certainly—there can't be as many disparate areas of high- and low-concentrations of food production—and one thing that will need to get crowded out is growing crops (especially food crops) for fuel. Biofuels, especially first-generation ones like corn ethanol—have proven pretty ineffective as efficient fuels, but it's a good example of the trade-offs necessary in a world of sustainable agriculture.

This plan also assumes global buy-in, which is easier said than done. The average American eats three cheeseburgers per week (along with a variety of other meaty treats), and ramping up sustainable agricultural practices in developing countries will require a big investment in labor, education, and oversight. Still, the point remains: It *can* be done, and if we can put a man on the moon, why can't we feed the world? Weekday vegetarians of the world, unite!

Organizations to Contact

Center for Science in the Public Interest (CSPI)

1875 Connecticut Ave. NW, Suite 300, Washington, DC   20009

(202) 332-9110 • fax: (202) 265-4954

Web site: www.cspinet.org

The Center for Science in the Public Interest is an advocate for nutrition and health, food safety, alcohol policy, and sound science. Founded by executive director Michael Jacobson and two other scientists, CSPI seeks to educate the public, advocate government policies that are consistent with scientific evidence on health and environmental issues, and counter industry's powerful influence on public opinion and public policies. CSPI publishes an award-winning newsletter, *Nutrition Action Healthletter,* and its Web site contains food and nutrition news and other information, including articles about the value of plant-based diets.

Farm Animal Rights Movement (FARM)

10101 Ashburton Lane, Bethesda, MD   20817

(888) 327-6872

e-mail: info@farmusa.org

Web site: www.farmusa.org

Farm Animal Rights Movement is a national public interest organization that promotes plant-based (vegan) diets to save animals, reduce global warming, conserve environmental resources, and improve public health. The group publishes an e-newsletter and its Web site provides information about vegetarianism, including a section on the environmental, health, animal rights, and other benefits of a vegetarian diet.

International Vegetarian Union of North America (VUNA)
c/o Vegetarian Society of DC, PO Box 4921
Washington, DC   20008
e-mail: vuna@ivu.org
Web site: www.ivu.org

The Vegetarian Union of North America is a network of vegetarian groups throughout the United States and Canada. Membership is open to groups; individuals can be supporters. As an independent regional organization of the International Vegetarian Union (IVU), VUNA serves as a liaison with the worldwide vegetarian movement and seeks to promote a strong, effective, cooperative vegetarian movement throughout North America. The VUNA Web site provides news, vegetarian recipes, and instructions for starting local vegetarian groups.

National Cattleman's Beef Association (NCBA)
5420 S Quebec St., Greenwood Village, CO   80111-1905
(303) 694-0305 • fax: (303) 694-2851
e-mail: cattle@beef.org
Web site: www.beef.org

The National Cattleman's Beef Association is the marketing organization and trade association for America's one million cattle farmers and ranchers. The group promotes beef consumption and its Web site contains a section on beef production that addresses such issues as the environment, animal welfare, and nutrition.

People for the Ethical Treatment of Animals (PETA)
501 Front St., Norfolk, VA   23510
(757) 622-PETA
Web site: www.peta.org

People for the Ethical Treatment of Animals is an animal rights and advocacy organization that focuses its attention on four areas of animal suffering: factory farms, laboratories, the clothing trade, and the entertainment industry. The group also works on a variety of other issues, including the cruel killing of beavers, birds, and other "pests," and the abuse of backyard dogs. PETA provides public education; conducts cruelty investigations, research, and animal rescue; promotes legislation; and sponsors special events, celebrity involvement, and protest campaigns. The PETA Web site is an excellent source of information about animal rights, factory farms, and other reasons for adopting a vegetarian diet.

TheVegetarianSite

PO Box 222, Glastonbury, CT   06033
(860) 519-1918
e-mail: inquiries@TheVegetarianSite.com
Web site: www.thevegetariansite.com

TheVegetarianSite.com was created in January 2000, with the goal of promoting and providing support for vegetarian or vegan lifestyles. It provides authoritative information on a wide array of topics, from health and nutrition, to animal rights issues, to agriculture, and the environment. In addition, the Web site offers complete online vegan shopping options. The group donates 10 percent of all sales every month to nonprofit vegetarian and animal rights organizations.

Vegetarian Resource Group (VRG)

PO Box 1463, Dept. IN, Baltimore, MD   21203
(410) 366-8343
e-mail: vrg@vrg.org
Web site: www.vrg.org

The Vegetarian Resource Group is a nonprofit organization dedicated to educating the public on vegetarianism and the interrelated issues of health, nutrition, ecology, ethics, and world hunger. In addition to publishing a quarterly magazine, the *Vegetarian Journal*, VRG produces and sells cookbooks, other books, pamphlets, and article reprints. The VRG Web site is also a good source of information about vegetarian nutrition and recipes.

Vegetarian Society of the United Kingdom

Parkdale, Dunham Road, Altrincham, Cheshire WA14 4QG
  England
0161 925 2000 • fax: 0161 926 9182
Web site: www.vegsoc.org

The Vegetarian Society of the United Kingdom is an educational charity promoting understanding and respect for vegetarian lifestyles. It offers advice about nutritional issues, environmental impact, and other aspects of vegetarianism. The group's Web site contains a wealth of information about vegetarianism—everything from statistics and information sheets on factory farming techniques to recipes and restaurant guides.

Bibliography

Books

Dawn Jackson Blatner	*The Flexitarian Diet: The Mostly Vegetarian Way to Lose Weight, Be Healthier, Prevent Disease, and Add Years to Your Life.* Columbus, OH: McGraw-Hill, 2008.
Susan Bourette	*Meat: A Love Story.* New York: Putnam Adult, 2008.
Gail A. Eisnitz	*Slaughterhouse: The Shocking Story of Greed, Neglect, and Inhumane Treatment Inside the U.S. Meat Industry.* Amherst, NY: Prometheus Books, 2006.
Hugh Fearnley-Whittingstall	*The River Cottage Meat Book.* New York: Ten Speed Press, 2007.
Jonathan Safran Foer	*Eating Animals.* New York: Little, Brown and Company, 2009.
Catherine Friend	*The Compassionate Carnivore: Or, How to Keep Animals Happy, Save Old MacDonald's Farm, Reduce Your Hoofprint, and Still Eat Meat.* Cambridge, MA: Da Capo Lifelong Books, 2009.
Scott Gold	*The Shameless Carnivore: A Manifesto for Meat Lovers.* New York: Broadway, 2008.

Suzanne Havala Hobbs	*Living Vegetarian For Dummies.* Hoboken, NJ: John Wiley & Sons, 2009.
Jennifer Horsman and Jaime Flowers	*Please Don't Eat the Animals: All the Reasons You Need to Be a Vegetarian.* Fresno, CA: Linden Publishing, 2006.
Karen Iacobbo and Michael Iacobbo	*Vegetarians and Vegans in America Today.* Santa Barbara, CA: Praeger, 2006.
Karen Iacobbo and Michael Iacobbo	*Vegetarian America: A History.* Santa Barbara, CA: Praeger, 2008.
Erik Marcus	*Meat Market: Animals, Ethics, and Money.* Cupertino, CA: Brio Press, 2005.
Sharalyn Pliler	*The Reluctant Vegetarian Cookbook: An Easy Introduction to Cooking Without Meat, Eggs, and Other Once-Favorite Foods and Discovering What Tastes Even Better.* Bloomington, IN: AuthorHouse, 2009.
Andrew Rimas and Evan Fraser	*Beef: The Untold Story of How Milk, Meat, and Muscle Shaped the World.* New York: Harper Paperbacks, 2009.
Stewart Rose	*The Vegetarian Solution: Your Answer to Heart Disease, Cancer, Global Warming, and More.* Summertown, TN: Book Publishing Company, 2007.

| Henry Stephens Salt | *The Logic of Vegetarianism: Essays and Dialogues.* Charleston, SC: BiblioBazaar, 2008. |

Peter Singer and Jim Mason — *The Way We Eat: Why Our Food Choices Matter.* Emmaus, PA: Rodale Books, 2006.

Tristam Stuart — *The Bloodless Revolution: A Cultural History of Vegetarianism from 1600 to Modern Times.* New York: W.W. Norton, 2007.

Bob Torres — *Making a Killing: The Political Economy of Animal Rights.* Oakland, CA: AK Press, 2007.

Periodicals

Sam Anderson — "Hungry? The Latest in a Bumper Crop of Books About the Ethics of Eating Animals," *New York Magazine,* November 1, 2009. http://nymag.com/arts/books/reviews/61735/.

Michael Bluejay — "Hitler Was Not a Vegetarian," *Vegetarian Guide,* 2009. http://michaelbluejay.com/veg/hitler.html.

John Cloud — "Study: Is Vegetarianism a Teen Eating Disorder?" *TIME,* April 7, 2009. www.time.com/time/health/article/0,8599,1889742,00.html.

Nathan Fiala   "How Meat Contributes to Global Warming," *Scientific American*, February 2009. www.scientificamerican.com/ article.cfm?id=the-greenhouse-hamburger.

Kathy Freston   "Vegetarian Is the New Prius," *The Huffington Post*, January 18, 2007. www.huffingtonpost.com/kathy-freston/ vegetarian-is-the-new-pri_b_39014.html.

Liz Galst   "Earth to PETA: Meat Is Not the No. 1 Cause of Global Warming. Yet Our Diet Is Cooking the Planet, and One Surprising Staple Turns Down the Heat," *Salon*, October 22, 2007. www.salon.com/news/feature/2007/ 10/22/peta/.

Brandon Keim   "Food Riots Begin: Will You Go Vegetarian?" *Wired Science*, April 21, 2008. www.wired.com/wiredscience/ 2008/04/food-riots-begi/.

Daniel Lazare   "My Beef With Vegetarianism," *The Nation*, February 5, 2007. www.thenation.com/doc/20070205/ lazare.

Christine Lennon   "Why Vegetarians Are Eating Meat," *Food & Wine*, August 2007. www.foodandwine.com/articles/ why-vegetarians-are-eating-meat.

Jim Motavalli   "Meat: The Slavery of Our Time," *Foreign Policy*, June 3, 2009. http://experts.foreignpolicy.com/ posts/2009/06/03/meat_the_slavery_ of_our_time.

Nicolette Hahn Niman — "The Carnivore's Dilemma," *New York Times*, October 30, 2009. www.nytimes.com/2009/10/31/opinion/31niman.html?_r=2&emc=etal.

Mark Oppenheimer — "Daddy Eats Dead Cows: Can a Meat-Loving Father Raise Vegetarian Children?" *Slate*, February 26, 2009. www.slate.com/id/2212193/.

Nina Planck — "Death by Veganism," *The New York Times*, May 21, 2007. www.nytimes.com/2007/05/21/opinion/21planck.html.

Natalie Portman — "Jonathan Safran Foer's *Eating Animals* Turned Me Vegan," *The Huffington Post*, October 27, 2009. www.huffingtonpost.com/natalie-portman/jonathan-safran-foers-iea_b_334407.html.

Steven Reinberg — "The Dark Side of Vegetarianism," *Health.com*, April 1, 2009. http://news.health.com/2009/04/02/the-dark-side-vegetarianism/.

Laura Shapiro — "Meat vs. Potatoes: The Real History of Vegetarianism," *Slate*, February 27, 2007. www.slate.com/id/2160746/.

Karen Springen — "Part-Time Vegetarians: Advocates Call It Flexitarianism, but Critics Say Being a Little Bit Vegetarian Is Like Being a Little Bit Pregnant," *Newsweek*, September 29, 2008. www.newsweek.com/id/161559.

Claire Suddath   "A Brief History of Veganism," *TIME*, October 30, 2008. www.time.com/ time/health/article/0,8599,1854996,00.html.

Jeanne Yacoubou   "The Vegetarian Solution to Water Pollution," *Vegetarian Journal*, 2009, iss. 1. www.vrg.org/journal/vj2009 issue1/2009_issue1_water_pollution.php.

Helene York   "A Defense of Meat Goes Too Far," *The Atlantic*, November 2, 2009. http://food.theatlantic.com/ sustainability/a-defense-of-meat -goes-too-far.php.

Index